Voices in Isolation:

4 Queer Plays at a Social Distance

By Owen Keehnen

Voices in Isolation: 4 Queer Plays at a Social Distance
ISBN 978-0-999217245
© 2021

Cover Design: Kirk Williamson
Author Photo: Israel Wright

**For Carl —
None of this would be possible
without you.**

Table of Contents

Preface
7

Sirens of the Belmont Rocks
9
Pansies on Parade
55
Presenting Wanda Lust
103
COVID Summer
151

About the Author
202

Preface

COVID and the effects of extended isolation have reshaped our lives and culture. The pandemic had a jarring impact on our relationships and our livelihoods. The virus forced us to rethink the guidelines of communication, interaction, and connection. We spoke through a mask and had virtual meetings. We were advised to shelter in place, and were told to keep six feet apart.

Voices in Isolation: 4 Queer Plays at a Social Distance explores performance and theater, reimagining LGBTQ drama in the era of COVID and beyond. Each of the four pieces in this collection explores the themes of queer visibility and queer history and has been staged and structured to reflect social distancing guidelines.

Social and personal distance is not a new theme in queer history. Most LGBTQ people have stood apart from mainstream society. Many were outcasts; others were closeted or had compartmentalized their desire. Those lives were lived at a distance, and they were important.

Voices in Isolation is an attempt to explore an added queer aspect to social distance in all its forms —from assimilation to separatism, from past to present, from onstage to offstage, and from whom we are to whom society defines us being.

At its core, *Voices in Isolation: 4 Queer Plays at a Social Distance* is a celebration of queer lives and queer history by reclaiming our stories and presenting them packaged for a new age. This gift is from the heart. In an era of uncertainty, passing on our history is more important than ever.

Sirens of the
Belmont Rocks

Cast

Voice A

Voice B

Voice D

Voice M

Voice P

Voice R

Voice V

Eddie Ramirez

The Staging / The Vibe

The stage is comprised of platforms of varying heights, preferably painted gray to resemble stones. Some of the "rocks" have been marked with graffiti and have artwork painted upon them. These are the Belmont Rocks. The rifle club is in the distance, painted on a backdrop. The backdrop sky is summer blue, some white clouds. Sun.

Seven characters lounge upon individual rocks. They are wearing speedos, swimwear, caftans, etc. The intended feel is 1970s queer beachwear.

The character of Eddie Ramirez is not a part of the opening setup. The character remains primarily offstage, with periodic appearances.

In the performance of the Sirens of the Belmont Rocks the actors may be seated, lounge on the stones as if tanning, or stand. However, each of the characters should remain on their specific platform / rock. There is no physical interaction.

The performers face the audience as though the audience is the lake. They are sirens singing out to sea — including the audience in their song.

Sirens of the Belmont Rocks

V:
It's good to be here again.

R:
And to be remembered.

A:
The way we are now was not what I expected.

B:
Neither being nor ghost.

P:
More something born of the sea.

V:
From a mist of clouds.

P:
We are what you see through the spray from the waves.

M:
A softness, fleeting as a thought.

A:
In some ways we carry on as expected.

B:
Our eternal now is an eternal then.

P:
No sudden wings and piety.

V:
All those poor holy rollers stuck waiting for the hereafter.

B:
That would make eternity seem like forever.

A:
Death is just Act II.

D:
With a complete costume change in between.

M:
Down to the bones.

V:
The toughest part in leaving is that to see Act II you have to leave the theater showing Act 1.

A:
Like a multiplex at the mall.

M:
Those aren't a thing anymore.

B:
Well pardon me Mr. died last year.

P:
Frankly, I am not surprised someone is thinking about me.

D:
(Turns to P)
Spoiler alert: Ego does not die with the body.

P:
(Back to D)
Bitch-craft is part of the great queer beyond as well.

A:
That's part of the queer over soul.

D:
And claws still grow after death.

M:
Is Jungle Red still a thing?

B:
Ruthless wit was a common language.

D:
A form of entertainment and protection all rolled into one.

M:
A recreational sport worthy of an event at the gay games.

A:
Those must be after my time.

D:
That code of camaraderie sharpened our wits. A quip was a kiss on the cheek. A well-timed witticism was how I told someone that I loved them.

P:
We showed our love in other ways as well.

B:
(Puts on sunglasses.)
No comment.

M:
Doggie. Missionary. Reverse Cowgirl. Don't call it sex addiction; call it a predilection for pleasure.

B:
(At M)
And you were partial to Chicken of the Sea if I recall.

M:
Among other things. I'm only picky when I have to choose.

V:
Me too. I did most anyone — anytime or anywhere. Why not? We all just wanted to celebrate pleasure.

D:
Nothing wrong with that.

V:
I tricked more than a few times on these very stones. These Rocks were baptized.

B:
There was a tearoom near Fullerton, and another one north at Belmont Harbor. There was my place, there was his place, and there was right then and there.

P:
Gay liberation and pride meant getting it on because we could and because it felt good.

D:
Herds of cattle have had less protein than this bunch.

A:
Sun makes a guy horny.

D:
(Carnival barker intonation.)
Get him while he's hot.

P:
Sex was in the air, carried on a mix of coconut oil, hormones, and weed.

M:
Most times I brought a magazine, but paid more attention to the constant cruising.

D:
Sex always seemed poised to happen.

A:
My back would get sunburnt because I would lie on my stomach for so long scoping out the action.

V:
Instead of a periscope we called him the Maryscope.

A:
(To V)
But never to my face.

V:
Well I'm not rude.

B:
I used to doze down by the waves. There was a special slanted rock near the water where I liked to lay. The limestone had a colorful grid pattern painted on it. I used to lie there and soak up the sun, along with a good amount of attention. By the end of the summer I was the color of a walnut.

A:
Everyone looks better with a tan. I baked until golden brown.

M:
Succulence by Coppertone.

D:
Ban de' Soliel

P:
Iodine and baby oil.

D:
We all had a preferred spot to be seen and to "work" on our tans.

P:
The grass was more social. The men stretched out on the actual Rocks tended to be more on the prowl.

D:
I preferred the Rocks.

M:
I liked the grass, but if I caught of whiff of something, I was ready to relocate to wherever the action was.

A:
I liked to sit on the top row and watch the action unfold.

R:
My spot was the middle rows of stones, near the bend to the south.

B:
Cocksucker cove.

R:
At that bend, the way the stones dipped made it easy to go unseen.

V:
Unless being seen was part of the scene.

P:
Or unless someone wanted to watch.

A:
Those days the men were everywhere, ready and available.

R:
And then there were men like . . .

B:
That
(He points. All heads turn.)

(Eddie Ramirez appears in silhouette at the top of the rocks straddling a bicycle.)

A:
Eddie Ramirez.

R:
The most beautiful man, pausing on his ride to survey his land.

M:
And trust me, he owned every inch of it.

P:
Eddie come over here, my back forty needs tending.

A:
You didn't summon Eddie Ramirez. That man was at no one's call. He chose you.

V:
Standing on those limestone slabs he looked like a god come to earth.

P:
Feet firm. Legs wide.

A:
Arms crossed over his chest.

M:
The fur on his body tapering down every speed bump of those tight muscles.

A:
And a bulge to make my mouth water.

M:
No one turned down Eddie Ramirez.

A
Every day I looked for him to ride over that ridge.

D:
I used to imagine what it was like to be that desired and to generate such lust.

B:
Knowing him wasn't easy.

R:
I knew him as well as anyone, and I barely knew him at all.

A:
That was one of the things that made him so sexy. He could be anything, or anyone. None of us cared.

M:
And he didn't care either.

V:
Even in the great beyond he's something greater, something beyond and aloof from what we are.

M:
Maybe he was an angel all along.

A:
Think outside the tabernacle. Maybe he was bigger than an angel. I thought of him as more a pagan deity ripe for worship.

P:
Eddie Ramirez was a name people carved into stone.

D:
I had so many fantasies about Eddie Ramirez that I crave a cigarette just thinking of him.

M:
Some of us had him in the flesh.

R:
Some more than once.

B:
I never had the nerve to approach him. I should have made a memory when I had the chance. But I was . . .

M:
Raised Catholic, we know.

A:
I swear to god, all you hear from Catholics in the afterlife are woulda, coulda, shoulda.

M:
The holy "shit" trinity.

V:
Eddie Ramirez may have been a god, but there were plenty of other male mortals to do.

(Eddie leaves on his bike.)

M:
Men who are ready, willing, and lubricated.

P:
The Rocks were a boot camp for tricking — observe, approach, connect.

A:
And squeal the deal.

B:
I had my fair share of all that. But more than the tricking at the Rocks, I remember the fun.

A:
Hanging out was the best part.

B:
Nothing to do. No responsibilities. No thought of the future, or tomorrow.

V:
It was just tan, dick, fun, repeat.

M:
Life was one long day in the sun.

A:
For many of us it is one endless night at a club as well.

B:
We explored it together. Became part of a great experiment together.

A:
Life was about having fun, partying, and hooking up. Jobs just paid the bills.

R:
The bars and the baths and the Rocks were where it all happened. Where we connected, and how we gained each other's trust.

B:
We had each other

D:
And I had the both of you. What's your point?

A:
(Turns to D)
If you would listen, I said we had each other. And I don't just mean like that.

D:
I listened to you all through the summer Roland, your ex, was dying. He had no one, so you stepped up. I always admired you for being his someone when he needed someone.

A:
And you listened.

D:
You needed to talk. The Rocks were your therapy. We baked together on these stones and got drunk or high and talked . . . and that's where you got some relief.

M:
We did what we could to help each other grieve, survive, and die.

A:
Roland wanted to be remembered as something more than another AIDS death.

P:
More were being diagnosed. More were dying every day.

A:
Roland was a writer who never finished his great American novel. He wanted to be remembered as witty and fun, as a pet owner, a snappy dresser, and the first queer to dive into Lake Michigan in the spring.

B:
Roland usually took the springtime plunge from somewhere near here.

A:
Until the year he died less a month before the spring thaw. We released balloons and spread his ashes on the day that the ice went out.

D:
Not long after, you were gone as well.

A:
I died at the end of summer. And I knew where I wanted my memorial.

D:
You were always prepared.

A:
On my deathbed I controlled what I could. A dozen friends were to meet after my passing at the Belmont Rocks to release some balloons and scatter my ashes.

V:
We made a chalk heart on the stone with his name inside. We held hands, stood in a circle, and shared memories of him.

A:
They swore they would never forget. Most have remembered their promise.

M:
That sort of promise haunts me. I have sworn to remember so many people that I know I've forgotten some of them.

A:
We were all in shock.

M:
This was our paradise.

B:
And suddenly it was paradise lost. Paradise bombarded.

R:
Fucking epidemic.

P:
Fucking epidemic.

V:
Fucking.

M:
Epidemic.

D:
Before then we were eager to carry on like there was no tomorrow.

B:
Why not? As long as there was plenty of penicillin the party need never end.

A:
AIDS ended the party. AIDS ended the dream.

M:
We left the discos, the bars, the bathhouses, and the Rocks and staggered into something right out of the Middle Ages.

B:
A disease was ravaging us. Making us unrecognizable.

V:
Turning us old and infirm. And being merciless with death.

A:
Overtaking every waking moment — casting a pall over all we had created.

B:
Sometimes we confided in one another and sometimes we distracted ourselves with one another.

M:
No one else understood what we were going through.

P:
Or didn't care.

A:
Some saw AIDS as convenient. Claims that it was God's will was pure petty hate draped in sacred robes.

V:
Life gets real when death gets real.

B:
More real for some than others.

(Action stops for a moment.
Light goes off on M.
Light goes off on V.
Light goes off on R.
Lights go off on P.
Lights off on A. B. D. and finally P.)

(The stage is black.)

(Eddie Ramirez appears on horizon for a moment. He is on his bike. He waits for the count of five seconds, and then rides away. With his departure, the lights slowly rise.)

R:
The isolation and fear could have torn us apart, destroyed us.

A:
Instead the nightmare brought us together.

B:
And the lesbians and allies stepped up.

M:
We are always at our best with a common enemy.

V:
The foundation of what we had built, in places like the bars and the Belmont Rocks, grew stronger.

A:
And community is the reason we remain here.

B:
At this queer space we called the Belmont Rocks.

R:
For now, eternity is tan, relax, chat, and cruise.

M:
But back in the day other things happened here too. Rallies happened at the Rocks. For years the Pride party after the parade was here for those who felt excluded by most community organized events.

R:
Meaning people of color.

A:
Gay groups and organizations had picnics and parties here. This was a place of celebration.

P:
Many of the bars had an annual cookout here that began at noon and moved back to the bar in the early evening.

M:
Those were another level of messy.

B:
But those parties, those groups were key for many of us.

A:
For some it was everything.

V:
We started to see the world a little differently, less apologetically.

M:
We wanted more than tolerance.

B:
We started to demand respect.

A:
We were done with the shit and the hassles and the raids.

V:
AIDS just put an exclamation point at the end of the sentence.

R:
This was a life or death for us, but most folks don't care if it's not about them.

A:
Others saw AIDS as not such a bad thing. After all, we topped America's Least Wanted List.

B:
The worst were those who hid behind religion.

M:
Claiming it was proof of God's disapproval or part of his fucked-up plan.

B:
Any religion lacking compassion is a confidence scam, a personality cult, a hate group, or any or all of the above.

M:
We didn't have time for any of that bullshit. We needed help.

V:
Our lives depended upon it.

P:
And many died because of it.

A:
With so much more to do in life.

R:
I was robbed of life at 25.

M:
37

R:
32

V:
In our prime.

M:
Being remembered brings us to these slanted limestone slabs, maybe because something bigger needs to be remembered. But we have egos too.

B:
Telling tales ignites the flash so we can be seen.

P:
Tasted.

M:
Smelled.

D:
Not touched.

R:
We can appear from the darkness like lightning bugs.

A:
The mermen of Cook County, rising when you think of us, submerging as the memory passes.

M:
Rising and submerging like the Rocks from season to season.

B:
We are summertime clouds that you can see if you take a moment and look overhead.

D:
We wait for you.

B:
Bulges baking in the sun.

P:
Popping fresh cakes so tasty.

D:
High and tight and ready for tonight.

A:
Just the thing to whet an appetite and make your knees go weak.

V:
Speedos in every color under the sun.

R:
Fluorescents.

M:
Rainbow shades.

D:
Animal prints.

V:
Basic black.

A:
Even white, if you were an exhibitionist.

D:
But a word to the wise: if you wear a white speedo you best have the goods to back it up.

P:
Some guys wore thongs.

M:
Cheek floss.

A:
Also in a variety of why-bother colors.

D:
Remember David who wore just a jockstrap? Half the time he was carrying the jock around in his hand anyway.

A:
I never complained. I recall David now that you recall him. Sometimes I think about those I'll never remember.

V:
Nick the Romanian.

B:
Stu and his Pomeranian.

P:
There was Kevin, Vladmir, Bob, and Juan the window dresser.

M:
Gabor, Seymour, Steve, Steven, and Steffan.

A:
And the guy who used a stick of butter for tanning oil.

D:
That was Larry. He was my dentist and even in his office he kind of smelled like an omelet. Great guy.

A:
There was Danny, Byron, Jimmy B., Scott, and Tom.

M:
The roll call rolls on, one upon another upon another.

V:
Endless wave upon endless wave.

R:
Some of my finest memories were of men whose names I never knew. Sometimes a single moment stays with you.

A:
He's talking about that cave man again. We need to set the stage.

M:
As the lake rose and fell and froze and thawed year in and year out the blocks rearranged. The stone slaps rose and fell and grew increasingly askew.

V:
Some rocks tumbled into the lake. Sometimes those rearrangements brought unexpected results.

R:
One summer those changes created a cave. You swam underwater, a moment's thrill for a foot or so, and then you came up inside. Strips of sunlight cut through the gaps between the limestone blocks above, giving this grotto an otherworldly glow. It gave me a dangerous thrill just being in there.

A:
The summer the cave appeared he took a boy there.

R:
I don't recall his name, but I remember our whispers and kisses in that sanctuary, the odd echoes, the light on the water, the tickle of his mustache, and the warmth of his mouth on mine. The waves lapped and popped. Never saw him after that day. I'd like to imagine that he is the one who thought me onto these stones. I like to think his memory of me is the reason I'm here.

P:
I met my partner here.

D:
You mean blew.

P:
They call blowjobs the gay handshake for a reason.

D:
I remember when you met, I was watching. I heard you say you loved his cock.

P:
He was exceptional, but that's not what I remember most. My favorite memory of him was when he painted our initials right here inside a heart and the word always. When he showed me it I cried. Sometimes corny is perfect.

D:
I never wanted a lover, a mate, or companion of any sort. I lived and died on my own and had plenty of fun along the way. There's something to be said for not having to answer to anyone. Freedom was enough for me.

R:
I met most of my friends here. Meeting someone outside a bar had a different feel.

B:
And the Rocks were open 24/7.

R:
Even though the lakefront supposedly closed at dusk.
(Leans forward and whispers.)
We didn't care. We all had years of experience doing things we weren't supposed to do.

M:
Breaking the law means nothing when the law has no respect for you.

B:
I remember coming here after the clubs closed. Pitch black, city lights behind us, endless stars over the lake, and a clear slice of moon. We called ourselves the children of the night.

R:
In the summertime we came here after the bars closed. We would sit and smoke and talk and carry on until dawn. Once the sun was set to break over the lake, we would grow silent and wait. That moment was everything.

M:
After the sun rose we usually passed out or went home. I like to think that maybe someone from my dawn brigade is remembering me, thinking about one of those mornings.

A:
If you came here at night in the winter, looked into the darkness, and listened to the creak and pop of the ice — you felt the magic.

M:
I didn't need the ice to feel the magic. I felt it every time I came here.

P:
Spread on a slab of stone like something at a buffet.

B:
That spread served plenty.

P:
Obvious jabs like that mean even less when you're dead.
(Points to B.)
The bottom line was I liked getting done. No crime there. I was young and cute, and I had plenty of guys who gladly obliged.

B:
The hardships of the great beauties.

P:
Not that I owe an explanation, but it wasn't really about the sex. I needed to be wanted and to see desire reflected in men's eyes.

A:
The Rocks were an ideal place to find secondhand self-esteem.

R:
And for the record — we all loved watching you being "adored". When you got done we moved in close.

M:
Voyeur and lookout were synonymous in those days.

B:
We were watching for cops.

A:
Some of us watched for cocks more than cops. And I won't apologize about that.

B:
When the cops were coming we still sent a signal.

V:
The police didn't need a reason to spoil the party. They got off on hassling us.

M:
Some had a chip.

D:
Or a secret.

V:
Or they had a point to make, or were having a bad day, or were overworked, or needed to round up more perverts to make quota. The reason wasn't as important as the fact that it was done.

M:
And got away with doing it.

A:
That kind wants life to be simpler again.

R:
Like a return to their days as bully of the schoolyard.

B:
Lives were being ruined, but for the cops and politicians it was business as usual.

M:
Elections brought a crackdown. A hard stance on vice sounds so good as part of a political platform.

V:
A tough stance on crime usually means they're talking about a certain kind of "criminal" (air quotes) . . . and we are a favorite scapegoat.

A:
They mostly left us alone at the Rocks. It was easier to shake down the bars for money.

V:
Speak for yourself, some of us they didn't leave alone.

D:
Some of us were harassed more than others.

M:
They used pure intimidation, a weak man's show of might.

A:
I watched a police raid at the Belmont Rocks. Nine police cars and a couple 3-wheelers roared over the grass. I thought it was something serious, but they came to arrest a tan twink in a speedo for selling sandwiches on city property without a license. They hauled him off to jail in his man bikini.

V:
They bullied because they could.

M:
Tried to shame us.

P:
And blame us for their misery.

M:
One time we saw the cruisers crossing the grass towards the Rocks, so a few of us hooked arms and did a kick line right towards the cop cars. We fucking Rocketted their ass.

B:
They had no place in our beach extravaganza.

R:
We were tired of being targeted.

P:
Sex had to be a part of it. A few of boys in blue cared a bit too deeply what the gay boys were doing — like they resented us for having the courage they lacked.

M:
It's basic psychology.

D:
Very basic.

A:
Oh, Officer Steel, that's quite a weapon.

V:
Strip search and handcuff me, Sargent Stud. And get real close to tell me all about my (sexy voice) violations.

M:
Making out with guys was all in the line of duty. Entrapment was the name of the game and if you got off before you pulled out the badge, so what.

B:
Let me zip up before I read you your rights.

M:
Us against them.

A:
But the harassment made us stronger.

B:
Another common enemy.

V:
They had no place here. The Belmont Rocks were ours.

M:
Since the mid 1960s we've made this undesirable strip of lakefront, this jumble of limestone blocks, and turned it into a cornerstone of our kingdom.

B:
We took this place and made it queer.

M:
(Sings)
On a queer day you could see forever.

A:
(To M)
You and Barbra even in the great beyond.

V:
I had a lambda beach towel and a speedo with the interlocking male symbols on the ass.

A:
For a day at the Rocks I took a bag with suntan oil, lube, a flask, a couple joints, a pad of paper in case I got inspired, and something to read.

R:
At the Rocks everyone brought something to read, or to pretend to read.

A:
I brought Genet.

B:
Baldwin

V:
Shirley MacLaine

M:
Gay Chicago and crossword puzzles.

P:
People.

A:
Another constant at the Rocks was music.

R:
A customized soundtrack for everyone.

D:
Transistor radios. Boom boxes, Tape decks.

R:
Margaritaville,

D:
Best of My Love by the Emotions.

V:
We are Family

M:
Saturday in the Park

A:
Band of Gold.

V:
The Hustle

A:
Smoke on the Water

B:
Hot Stuff.

P:
We all had our songs, our jams, and our genres. I was all about going to the discos; wearing tight clothes, getting a buzz on, and dancing. I loved the feel of my business packed into a tight pair of pants.

B:
Horny as fuck because it was Wednesday night.

A:
Or Thursday

V:
Or Friday

M:
Or Saturday, Sunday, Monday, or Tuesday.

R:
The Rocks were my recovery zone from the night before.

M:
Hangover Sunday was most every day of the week there. Our sweat was probably 60 proof.

P:
Remember meeting at the Rocks with an enormous thermos of Bloody Marys to share tales from those nights of whistles, confetti cannons, and recreational drugs galore.

A:
Toot toot heyyy . . .

B:
Beep beep.

M:
Disco nights of flashing lights and sirens like us. Flashes from the past. Sirens calling from our stones eager to be remembered if only for a moment.

V:
We are a Greek chorus.

D:
You got that right.

B:
We are chorus boys on these stones.

P:
Part of some elaborate dance routine in a Busby Berkeley musical.

D:
Golddggers of 1988, wisecracking our way into the great beyond.

M:
Boys of the chorus, spreading our legs in synch to a song with a snazzy title like The Boy in the Razzle Dazzle Bikini. The song isn't as important as our synchronized movement.

A:
We dazzled and shone, lived and died together.

M:
And here were are — together again.

V:
We joke and we snipe, but we have each other.

D:
The hereafter is basically the Golden Girls with a jumbo lanai.

A:
And better clothes.

R:
There are certainly worse things. And honestly, few better.

B:
Paradise is our memory of each other, our memory of ourselves, and the joy of being remembered — knowing someone thought us here.

A:
(Abruptly turns to a person in the audience)
Maybe it is you who thought us and brought us.

D:
(Does same.)
Or you.

B:
Maybe you recognize someone in us, someone who keeps you here, and keeps us here.

R:
Someone gone, but not really.

P:
Someone whose memory comes to mind when you're tooling down Lake Shore Drive and happen to look over.

V:
Or cleaning out a junk drawer and you find a photo.

B:
Or a book of matches with a trick's number inside.

A:
Or Netflix is showing Outrageous Fortune and you remember going with the gang to see it at the Village Theatre on Clark Street, and how two of you attended in Bette Midler drag.

P:
Memories are doorways. One minute we are here, and the next we're not here.

B:
The afterlife is a very part-time job, like only working on-call for super special catering gigs.

A:
You don't remember us much.

B:
Less than you would think.

V:
Everyone is so busy.

M:
But no one wants to be forgotten. Being remembered anchors us for a bit. Otherwise we come and go like air currents.

V:
Part of something and then . . . not.

P:
Like a big cosmic lava lamp.

A:
We are this one and then that one. We are no one and everyone.

M:
We are scraps of memory snagged on a branch.

A;
Our voices, our stories, and our lives woven in a tapestry of this place.

D:
Fates as well as sirens.

M:
Muses too. Notes poised to be played.

P:
(Stands and walks to the edge of their platform)
I remember what it was like to walk the top row of stones, from one end to the other. Checking it all out. Checking them all out. Being checked out. The rocks dipped and rose and curved, so there was always the possibility of happening upon some juicy surprise.

P:
I never tired of the energy here. I felt it pulling me as I took the underpass by Diversey Harbor, around the gun club, past the statue, and towards the lake. Men standing on the top row of Rocks. Watching. An electric charge in the air.

B:
An erotic charge.

A:
Like the walls of an electric anus.

(All turn to look at A. Pause)

A:
I mean, we are all pulled into the nucleus of this cell.

V:
Atmospheric Viagra

B:
A deep sniff of poppers that you feel down to your rocks.

P:
I was hooked from the start. I went there the next day, and the next, and many days after. The Rocks were an ideal blend of risky and safe.

B:
I get emotional about it.

R:
My best memories of the Belmont Rocks are simple: a cooler, a guy, some Coppertone, and a joint — lying in the sun, lightly touching, getting horny as fuck.

B:
We all loved some afternoon delight.

A:
Whore your way to a glowing complexion.

M:
Remember the kid who sold oregano and told everyone it was pot? Walking along that top row of stones calling, Joints. Joints. Joints.

Nobody bought a joint from the kid more than once. Whenever someone asked what kind of pot it was, that was his answer — Afternoon Delight.

R:
A bogus joint was a rite of passage.

V:
Life was a rite of passage.

P:
Maybe this afterlife is a rite of passage as well. No one knows if the curtain will fall on all this as well. There has been talk of Act III.

B:
Maybe this is all there is, but it seems there has to be an elsewhere, a place where people go when they cease to be remembered.

R:
No one is remembered forever unless you're Elvis or Jesus or Marilyn.

A:
That takes marketing.

M:
If this is all there is, if this is the big eternal, I'm fine with spending it here with lovers and friends, and having time measured in the lapping of waves.

B:
There's time to think here.

D:
I used to think if I had it all to do over I would do so much differently, but then I realized that I did everything I did for a reason.

A:
The notion of eternity on these slanted stones turns everyone into a philosopher.

D:
These stones are warm with our stories. These stones marked by art, romance, and death.

P:
Marked with devotion and defiance in an open-air gallery all our own.

R:
Someone painted a picture of me here once. Ted had a kind of Picasso style, but I could tell it was me. The figure had my tattoo. We lasted a couple months, but his rock art lasted a couple summers. Eventually the lake wore away the top layer of stone. By then Ted was gone too. The last summer he was alive he never came to the Rocks.

B:
Kaposi's is not a great look in a speedo.

D:
Or a caftan and turban.

B:
The beauty that once opened doors now kept him behind one.

V:
The virus turned many into hermits.

A:
And the isolation caused by the illness was worse than the illness itself.

R:
One day, when Ted felt up to it, we came here and sat a while. He was smiling. Sickness was taking him over. The virus was attacking his brain. He was so easily agitated. But that day at the Rocks, he was content for a while. We sat on the top row for 45 minutes and watched

the boys. He hadn't left his apartment in weeks. When the sky clouded and the wind picked up, Ted started to get frustrated, a side effect of his medication.

A:
Being pissed off was a side effect of the virus and all the bullshit that came along with it.

R:
But that day at the Belmont Rocks, at least for a while, Ted was content.

P:
He watched us warming ourselves in the sun, holding the heat. Ted was sick, but he wasn't dead. Who doesn't like a sexy little show?

R:
The virus was crystallizing his lungs, but at the Rocks he had found the freedom to breath. But when the clouds came, the warmth from his comrades was no longer enough.

M:
Ted lived on the 16th floor of a high rise on Sheridan.

R:
You could see the Rocks from his living room window — beyond the glass, beyond Lake Shore Drive. His telescope was still aimed at the Rocks when we went to clean out his apartment a couple weeks later.

B:
He knew how important it was to have a place to be ourselves.

D:
Or someone else entirely if that was what you were into.

R:
He saw how important it was to be together in the sunshine at a time when our bars still had blackened windows.

M:
I liked the Rocks better than the bars.

R:
Much better.

V:
They complimented one another. So many days started at the Rocks and ended in the bars.

D:
Life is a circle, at least socially.

A:
The Belmont Rocks were a part of who we became. An experiment in stone. A queer temple for worship of the water, the sun, each other, and ourselves.

V:
A shrine to the sanctity of friendship and community and worship of the flesh.

P:
Skin was always "in" at the Rocks.

(Eddie Ramirez appears at the top of the platform. He is on his bike. The light on him slowly dims and he rides away.)

D:
Some of us were only here briefly.

M:
My stomach dropped the moment I was diagnosed, but I was one of the lucky ones, until my luck ran out.

V:
I could not get past the unfairness. Acceptance never happened for me. All I kept thinking was, Why me? I never made peace, why should I?

D:
My cause of death was a diseased society.

B:
My cause of death was insufficient insurance.

P:
I died of bureaucratic indifference.

V:
I prayed not to die, but I died anyway.

A:
I chanted myself into the hereafter.

M:
I worked on loving myself, forgiving myself, releasing guilt, mirror affirmations, sage and dream catchers and a jelly jar of crystals, but all that meant nothing to the virus.

A:
But it meant something to you.

R:
Death, God, government, and insurance companies didn't care how much you wanted to live.

P:
In the end life is a memory bank — not a bank for storage but a bank of stones to lounge upon for all eternity.

M:
Who knew that those afternoons at the Rocks were a preview of things to come?

B:
We all have a spot here, a place in the sun.

P:
Though people don't appear here as much anymore and I worry one day even the Rocks will cease to be remembered.

M:
By then we shall be elsewhere as well.

V:
Or maybe not. I'm here because this was happiness was for me.

D:
In the end all that matters is freedom, belonging, and a place to call our own.

(Lights dim upon the characters. Eddie Ramirez appears at the top of the Belmont Rocks. Looks for a moment. Sighs. And rides away.)

Pansies on Parade

Cast

Gladys Bentley

Rae Bourbon

Bothwell Brown

Jean Malin

Karyl Norman

Bert Savoy

Queero

Queerette

Announcer

The Staging / The Vibe

The lighting for Pansies on Parade is dark and smoky. Shadowed. Decadent. The stage should feel as though the audience is seated in a nightclub that is equal parts glitz and grime. Hanging at the back of the stage is a backdrop that reads, Pansies on Parade.

Gladys stands at a microphone front and center.

A smaller elevated stage stands to the side. This stage is decorated more crudely with tinsel curtains and harsh footlights. This is where the pansy performers do their numbers.

Beside the platform is messy dressing room. Makeup mirrors, makeup, clothes, etc. are strewn about. In the dressing room five pansies sit at a social distance of six feet from each other, each busy preparing to go on.

Seated at a two top cocktail table is at the side of the stage are Queero and Queerette, who add commentary over their martinis.

Announcer is behind the curtain.

Pansies on Parade

(LIGHTS DIM AND THEN RISE. There is a brief jazzy overture. The lights come up. Queero and Queerette are already seated at their cocktail table.)

Announcer:
The Imperial Club in the bohemian capital of the great beyond extends a fey fairyland 'HALLO' " to one and all for an evening of gender blending and fun. The master of ceremonies this evening is the bull dagger who put the hot in hot Harlem, Gladys Bentley.

Gladys:
Welcome one and all to a place where things are a little wilder . . . and where the growls go a bit lower. Leave your inhibitions with the cupcake at the coat check, because we do not have room for anyone's baggage on the premises. We are hear to leave all that behind.

(Gladys Bentley performs The Worried Blues. Performer should flirt openly with females in the audience.)

Gladys:
Tonight we have a little show for you.
(To a woman in the audience)
And you got a show for me later tonight too.
(To crowd)
But that is another affair. First let me introduce our cast.
These two are such fixtures at this club I thought their asses were glued to the stools. Our favorite off stage fairies, Queero and Queerette . . . though I don't think they ever learned the meaning of the phrase off stage.

(Queero and Queerette lift their glasses to the audience.)

Gladys:
Tonight we have a show with a lineup that you're not likely to forget.

Queero:
Until you see them all again at the central police station after a vice sweep.

Gladys:
May I present the banter, the canter, and the fairyboy frolic of Mr. Jean Malin,

(Malin comes out. Waves. Curtsies. Enters the dressing room.)

Bert Savoy

(Comes out. Blows a kiss. Blows a second kiss, enters dressing room.)

Rae Bourbon

(Comes out. Blows, Rises, Slinks to the dressing room.)

Karyl Norman

(Comes out. Full spin. One pose. Two Pose. Goes to Dressing room.)

And Bothwell Brown

(Comes out. Cruises the audience before heading to the dressing room.)

Gladys:
Ladies, and gentleman, fairies and marys, daggers and drags, and all stops between and beyond. Tonight we present a tangy footlight frolic we like to call, Pansies on Parade. As is my way, I will be taking charge of the ladies tonight.

Queero:
Femme, Belle, Punk.

Queerette:
Queen, Fairy, Sissy, Queer . . .

Queero:
Invert.

Queerette:
Pervert.

Queero:
We've been called everything but sir.

Queerette:
Our skin is thicker than an elephant's hide.

Queero:
Impenetrable.

Queerette:
You can't get under it.

Queero:
You learn that skill mighty fast when you fall out of favor.

Queerette:
But for a while things were so different. For three solid years, they adored us.

Queero:
And with good reason. We made the mundane sparkle.

Queerette:
We were the bubbles in a glass of champagne.

Queero:
Decadent.

Queerette:
The perfect tonic in a cynical age.

Queero:
They put us on the stage, and I'm not talking about the one that leaves at noon.

Queerette:
The pansies were front and center and bringing in the crowds.

Queero:
A taste of gay Paree and old Berlin.

Queerette:
Witty, risqué, continental.

Queero:
Off stage we were in vogue too. Every high society hostess knew that a pansy or two was an absolute must at any decent sized urban gathering or party.

Queerette:
To succeed both on or off the stage, a brillatined dandy had to be sharp and witty, confident and fey.

Queero:
The rightful bastards of Oscar Wilde.

Queerette:
The big build up started with Jean Malin. He helped ignite the Pansy Craze.

Gladys:
Jean was a gay boy from Brooklyn. As a teen he started winning prizes for his costumes at the Manhattan drag balls of the 1920s. By his late teens he was a veteran Broadway chorus boy.

Queero:
A reviewer of his performance in Sisters of the Chorus described Jean as "husky but dainty."

Gladys:
Before he turned 20, Malin was headlining at some of the top clubs in Greenwich Village where he was billed as six feet of attitude and lisp.

Malin:
Guilty as charged.

Announcer:
Though considered a "drag artist," Jean Malin did not appear on stage in female attire.

Gladys:
Jean's act was to be as flamboyant, as effeminate, and as queer as a man can be while wearing a tuxedo.

Malin:
I impersonated the divas of the day, Gloria Swanson, Theda Bara,

Queero:
He didn't need a wig to do any of the ladies. He did it with inflection, a shift in posture, or the tilt of his head. The crowds went wild.

Queerette:
The people loved Jean.

Queero:
They loved the pansies.

Queerette:
For a while they couldn't get enough.

Queero:
But some critics were brutal when reviewing the fairy cabarets.

Malin:
They didn't just hate the act; they hated me.

Queero:
The pansies threatened their masculinity.

Queero:
We were confident, and many thought we should be ashamed. The reviews were often not about what we did but about who we are.

Queerette:
One reviewer called Jean Malin, "a baby-faced lad who lisped and pressed his fingers into his thighs"

Malin:
Let him eat crow. I'm the one in lights on the marquee. It's me that people are coming to see.

Queerette:
Another critic was more direct, saying, "This latest innovation of the stage sickens me."

Malin:
Then he referred to me as a young man who walks with four fingers to my lips.

Queero:
What does that even mean?

Malin:
It probably means he would kill me if he could. But I bet that know-it-all critic failed to mention in his diatribe that I was the highest paid nightclub entertainer of 1930.

Announcer:
Malin's stage persona and audience rapport was of a queer and swishy delight and impeccably urbane emcee. The pansies even hailed "La Malin" as their queen.

(Queero & Queerette raise glassed to him.)

Queero:
I would bow, but I don't do that.

Queerette:
Jean Malin was in the columns every other day.

Queero:
Some of it was good, some not so good.

Queerette:
A real celebrity.

Queero:
And the headlines were as much about who he was as what he did.

Queerette:
La Malin made headlines when he punched a heckler.

Malin:
He was giving me lip all night. The popular press acted like a pansy could never throw a punch. Those dolts never played the dives I've had to play. Most times I try to shut up those pie-eyed jokers with a comeback, but this time I had enough.

Queero:
Jean Malin was full of surprises.

Announcer:
Despite an obvious fondness for men, Jean Malin married a woman.

Gladys:
Talk about a surprise headline!

Queero:
Some called it a stunt.

Announcer:
And they had good reason. In 1936, five years after the wedding, and three years after Jean Malin's death, his widow Lucille was convicted of operating a brothel. Six years later, she was arrested for the same offense.

Queerette:
(Eyeing the audience)
Don't judge.

Gladys:
All the damn gossip. Everybody is getting ahead of things.

Announcer:
In the early 1930s, Jean Malin was touring coast to coast, New York, Boston, Miami, Chicago, Detroit, Los Angeles.

Malin:
And drawing record crowds at every damn show.

Queero:
And naturally, Hollywood took notice.

Announcer:
Jean Malin made a handful movies including Dancing Lady with Joan Crawford. In the film he played a pansy performer and sang Frankie and Johnny in Mae West drag.

Malin:
I could have done it in my sleep.

(West's Frankie and Johnny playing low)

Queero:
Once they caught wind of it, morality groups had a fit.

Queerette:
Churches and community organizations denounced Malin, the studio,

and the "plague of perverts" walking the streets in towns across the country.

Queero:
They said his role in the film was not a performance, but an "abomination."

Malin:
And they said it without seeing the movie.

Queero:
Morality groups fanned the flames.

Queerette:
Malin's touring train was mobbed on more than one occasion.

Malin:
A nun went on a hunger strike to protest the ongoing acceptance of sissies like me.

Queerette:
Sister Go Mind Yourself.

Malin:
They called our kind unseemly and unspeakable and claimed we were (finger quotes) "everywhere."

Queero:
The studio head supposedly admitted that personally, he was "disgusted" by Gene Malin and his performance.

(Frankie and Johnny stops playing.)

Gladys:
The small minds won out in the end.

Announcer:
Jean Malin's footage was deleted from the movie and his scenes were reshot with a more "suitable" actor.

Queero:
Someone less flamboyant.

Jean Marin:
I was still drawing crowds, still making money hand over fist. I wasn't happy being replaced, but they still paid me. I tried not to let it bother me. I tried, but even with a hide that stuff stings.

Queerette:
Some saw the writing on the wall.

Queero:
Others didn't see it coming at all.

Malin:
There were other studios, other pictures. I made a movie called Double Harness with Connie Bennett.

Queero:
His role in the picture was met with a similar moral outage.

Queerette:
And that movie was scrapped as well.

Queero:
Two expensive mistakes for a studio to make.

Announcer:
One high ranking studio executive reportedly said that gentleman of Malin's sort has no business being on the screen, or anywhere.

Malin:
Which sounds to me like a call for lynching.

Queero:
We were called a national disgrace, a menace.

Queerette:
They said things like, I would not want to sit in a dark theater beside something, not someone, something like that.

Queero:
They said we could not be trusted.

Queerette:
Which meant they couldn't trust themselves.

Queero:
Predatory.

Malin:
I was called a threat to manhood, to the family, and to all things decent. Little old me.

Queerette:
The boys in charge of the dream factory agreed that the American people weren't ready.

Queero:
Especially when the decency groups start tossing around threats and words like boycott.

Malin:
The crowds still loved me.

Queerette:
Some of the crowds anyway.

Queero:
Until they were taught otherwise.

Queerette:
Some felt a moral obligation to purge us from society

Queero:
And if that wasn't possible, it was best to keep us hidden and ashamed.

Queerette:
We did what we had to. We disappeared.

Gladys:
Excuse me. You two need to mind what's going on up here. You're ahead of the story again.

Announcer:
Near the end of the Pansy Craze, Jean Malin recorded two of his songs; one of them was "That's What's the Matter With Me."

(Play snippet of That's What's the Matter With Me: 5 seconds.)

Gladys:
The way it all ended was terrible.

Announcer:
Jean Malin was killed in a freak accident on Aug 10, 1933. He had just given his "farewell performance" at the Ship Café in Venice, CA.

Queero:
Literally, it was his farewell performance. Above the club that night was a banner that read, the Last Night of Jean Malin.

Queerette:
That sign was a sign.

Malin:
Now that was a party! After the festivities, I staggered out to my sedan with my "extremely close friend" Jimmy Forlenza, and another pal, actress Patsy Kelly. Patsy was always a lot of laughs.

Queero:
She was about as out as a dyke in the spotlight could be. Patsy was just finding fame as a wisecracking character actress.

Announcer:
The night of his farewell performance, Jean Malin confused the gears when he shifted. The car lurched in reverse, splintering the wood, and plunging off the pier into several feet of water.

Malin:
I can't even drive straight.

Announcer:
Forienzo was thrown free of the car and sustained minor injuries. Miss Kelly was pulled from the wreck and rushed to the hospital for x-rays. Memories of the accident would haunt her for decades.

Malin:
I was happy no one else was injured too badly.

Announcer:
Jean Malin was pinned behind the steering wheel of the submerged vehicle. .

Queero:
The stuff of nightmares.

Announcer:
Jean Malin, the Queen of the Pansies, was dead at age 25. He is buried at Most Holy Trinity Cemetery in Brooklyn.

Queero:
Not just holy, but most holy.

Queerette:
Fitting for La Malin. Jean Malin was extra, he was a comet that streaked through the sky . . .

Queero:
As though greased with Crisco.

Malin:
What did I know? I was a fat queer kid from Brooklyn suddenly on top of the world. I was making cash hand over fist and having the time of my life. I had 500 people at my 23rd birthday party. Not many people can say that.

Queero:
He was beloved.

Malin:
And I could have made them love me even more.

Gladys:
Jean Malin died just as the pansy craze was coming to an end.

Malin:
Lesson number one from my vaudeville days is to know the importance of a well-timed exit.

Queero:
For some the Pansy Craze died that night.

(Gasps and noises of offense come from the dressing room pansies.)

Gladys:
And now, Jean Malin, singing one of the numbers that caused a sissy sensation, That's What's the Matter With Me.

(Malin performs the number.)

Queero:
Like a fine wine.

Queerette:
That has sat open a few years.

(To audience)

Queero:
Don't mind our pansy playing.

Queerette:
We are bitchy and silly.

Queero:
Madcap and glib and brimming with wit.

Queerette:
The most social of all social creatures.

Queero:
We all fancied ourselves in the know.

Queerette:
Powdered, perfumed, and ready to star in our own revue.

Malin:
I may have been the headliner, but my career was possible because of acts like Bert Savoy.

Announcer:
Bert Savoy was born in Boston in 1876, though he often claimed to be at least a dozen years younger.

Queero:
Girl, 12 years.

Bert Savoy:
In the right lighting.

Queerette:
That's not shaving off years — that's gouging off years.

Announcer:
Cross-dressing vaudevillian Bert Savoy began his drag career at age 14 as a taxi dancer.

Queero:
(To audience)
A taxi dancer was a gal for hire as a dance partner at music halls.

Queerette:
Only Bert was a dance partner with a little something extra.

Queero:
That took some guts.

Bert Savoy:
I had to eat.

Queero:
A taxi dancer is the kind of job that makes you come up with another plan.

Bert Savoy:
On my feet in heels all day, no thank you. I wasn't going to get those ugly veins.

Gladys Bentley:
Bert still felt his drag.

Queerette:
And was naturally theatrical.

Queero:
And soon an idea came to him.

Announcer:
Bert Savoy added some beads and bangles, a tarot deck, and crystal ball hung out a shingle and became, Madame Veen, mystic, seer, and fortuneteller.

Queero:
Bert was good at it.

Bert Savoy:
I see a tall dark, handsome man in your future.

Queero:
What, just the one?

Queerette:
The line is from an old Mae West routine.

Queero:
Much of Mae West's material was courtesy of Bert Savoy.

Gladys:
Again you two are going way ahead on things. Do you think we can continue the story now?

(Queero and Queerette pause and nod for things to continue.)

Announcer:
By 1905 Bert Savoy was described as an "outrageous vaudevillian" when he wed costume designer Anna Krehmker.

Bert Savoy:
What was I thinking?

Queero:
She was a costume designer, maybe he was thinking, Free Gowns.

Queerette:
Krehmker eventually filed for divorce.

Bert Savoy:
Performing was my true love.

Queero:
In addition to cock.

Announcer:
By 1914, Bert Savoy had teamed with Jay Brennan and became the Society Jesters.

Queero:
Apparent Bert "met" Brennan on a streetcar.

Bert Savoy:
When I asked him if he was a fan of Browning, naturally I meant the great poet, Robert Browning.

Announcer:
During this era, browning was also slang for anal sex.

Bert Savoy:
At any rate it proved a perfect icebreaker.

Announcer:
In the act, the dapper "straight man" Jay Brennan chatted with Bert Savoy who was wearing a bright red wig and the latest Paris frocks.

Gladys Bentley:
He was having the time of his life on that stage.

Bert Savoy:
Once I had the outfit on my back and I looked the part, I knew the character.

Announcer:
A master of camp and pantomime, Bert Savoy built his line chatter around gossiping with an imaginary girl friend named Margie. He would end the scene walking off stage, waving a chiffon handkerchief, and shouting to Brennan:

Bert Savoy:
"You don't know the half of it, Dearie."

Queero:
He minced his way to stardom.

Bert Savoy:
I took that stereotype all the way to the bank. Why shouldn't I? I knew what it was to be poor and this was a whole lot better.

Announcer:
The act was a sensation. The Society Jesters headlined in the Ziegfeld Follies of 1918 as well as the Greenwich Village Follies of 1920 and 1922. Though drag had always been a part of vaudeville—drag was not perceived as "gay" until Bert Savoy came along.

Bert Savoy:
How's that for having an impact, dearie?

Queero:
Pure camp on and off the stage.

Bert Savoy:
I couldn't be any way other than what I was. I didn't have the mask that a lot of fellows did. I couldn't be queer one minute and a straight arrow the next. Being funny saved my ass.

Announcer:
Other female impersonators of the day, like the sensation, Julian Eltinge, claimed cross-dressing was just an act. Off stage, Eltinge was very concerned with pushing his virility and making it clear that he was a cigar-smoking male who engaged in "traditional male" activities.

Queerette:
If you want to butch it up by tinkering with your Rolls while chomping on a cigar, feel free.

Queero:
But he had a theater named after him. He crossed over into the movies.

Gladys Bentley:
Sometimes you do what you have to if you want to get things.

Bert Savoy:
Funny thing is, Julian Eltinge may have smoked cigars and fixed cars for the camera, but he never married. I did.

Announcer:
Bert Savoy's skits contributed to popular culture with phrases such as

Bert Savoy:
"You slay me."

Malin:
That was you?

Bert Savoy:
That was I.

Announcer:
Bert was also largely the inspiration behind the "persona" of Mae West.

Gladys Bentley:
The rolling West strut and sexual bravado were Bert Savoy.

Announcer:
Two of Bert Savoy's routines were preserved for posterity on a rare 1923 recording made shortly before his death.

Queero:
Spoiler alert.

Queerette:
(To Gladys Bentley.)
That was the announcer that time. So you can't blame us.

Announcer:
On June 26, 1923, Savoy and two friends were walking along the Long Island shore, watching an upcoming storm roll in when a thunderclap prompted Bert Savoy to put one hand on his hip and supposedly squeal:

Bert Savoy:
(Hand on hip).
Ain't Miss God cuttin' up somethin' awful?

Announcer:
The moment the words were out of his mouth, Bert Savoy was struck dead by a bolt of lightning.

Bert Savoy:
No comment.

Queerette:
You really can't write stuff like that.

Queero:
Even for vaudeville schtick.

Announcer:
Bert Savoy is buried in Woodlawn Cemetery in the Bronx. His grave bears the words,

Bert Savoy:
"He Made the World Laugh."

Queerette:
Right up to the final curtain.

Queero:
Accompanied by thunderous applause.

Bert Savoy:
(Takes a bow, waves, and leaves the stage saying his catchphrase)
You don't know the half of it, Dearie.

Announcer:
Another reigning queen of the Pansy Craze was Rae Bourbon, who rode the sissy wave to popularity and, unlike many of his contemporaries, continued to entertain for decades afterward. Like most of the other pansies, Bourbon was a veteran of vaudeville. He was also a protégée of Mae West.

Queerette:
She didn't mince, but at lot of Mae West was pure pansy.

Rae Bourbon:
I grew up in nowhere Texas, wanting to be somewhere. At night the sky was full of stars, but the rest of the time Texas was a whole lot of nothing.

Queerette:
Especially for a boy with stars in his eyes.

Queero:
And a taste for something more.

Rae Bourbon:
I was eager to be a movie star, to have my name in lights, and to sign autographs for fans.

Announcer:
Desperate to get to Hollywood, Rae Bourbon entered a contest that Paramount Pictures was holding to find the Starlet of Tomorrow.

Rae Bourbon:
Fate stepped in and was telling me what I had to do. I got all dolled up sent my picture off to Paramount, and I won the goddamn contest.

Announcer:
First place was a trip to Hollywood and a screen test for Paramount.

Rae Bourbon:
Everything that I wanted was coming to be. It was like a dream. The studio paid my way out there and I was ready.

Announcer:
The PR stunt backfired. When the boys at Paramount publicity realized that a man in drag had won the contest. The deal was off. No screen test.

Queerette:
Some poor PR schmuck probably lost a job.

Rae Bourbon:
They treated me like dirt, but at least it got me out of Texas and paid my way to wonderland.

Announcer:
By 1932, Rae Bourbon was working full-time as a female impersonator. Even after the twilight of the Pansy Craze, he continued to headline at gay clubs nationwide.

Rae Bourbon:
I had a reputation.

Queero:
Off stage as well as on.

Announcer:
As a pansy Bourbon was a bit different. He wasn't always the most polished or witty. In fact, Rae was pretty risqué, and often crass.

Rae Bourbon:
Name me a longtime club comic who isn't. The life toughens you. If you're not tough, you're not going to make it. And I didn't come here to fail.

Gladys Bentley:
Bourbon was willing to do most anything for a laugh.

Rae Bourbon:
To keep packing the house you have to hustle. You have to keep them interested. Nothing comes for free and nothing is forever.

Queerette:
Rae knew how to play the game and he loved publicity.

Rae Bourbon:
I had a scrapbook of clippings.

Queero:
All sorts of things.

Rae Bourbon:
Once I was arrested on live radio. You can't buy publicity like that.

Queero:
Rae was always working. He toured with Mae West in her shows Catherine Was Great in 1944 and Diamond Lil in 1948.

Announcer:
After touring with West, Bourbon worked for years at Finocchio's drag club in San Francisco.

Bert Savoy:
I never had a steady job before, and I never did again. Call me a masochist, but I liked being on the road.

Announcer:
Touring the country. Bourbon was charged with female impersonation in a number of places.

Queero:
He had quite a record.

Rae Bourbon:
Seattle, Miami, El Paso, New Orleans . . . My rap sheet was getting so long you could wrap a couple fish with it.

Queero:
And some critics did just that.

Rae Bourbon:
I listen to the folks who come to the show, not the critics. And the folks who come to my show wanted something, and I decided to give it to them.

Announcer:
Rae Bourbon released dozens of albums, becoming the most prolific female impersonator of the period in regards to recording.

Rae Bourbon:
They were 78s on my own UTC label.

Queero:
UTC isn't a urinary tract thing.

Gladys Bentley:
That stood for Under the Counter.

Rae Bourbon:
Where record stores usually kept my recordings.

Gladys Bentley:
Things were a hell of a lot worse for the queers in the 1950s than they ever were in the 1930s.

Rae Bourbon:
I recorded about 10 hours worth of my material. That was how I would survive. I was leaving my legacy.

Announcer:
Despite his very public act and material, Rae Bourbon was vague or elusive when asked about his sexuality.

Queero:
Perhaps he was closeted, or worried about the law. Rae was arrested for keeping his mouth open enough times to know when to keep his mouth shut.

Announcer:
Bourbon had relationships with men and women. He married twice, and fathered a son.

Rae Bourbon:
And why shouldn't I? I wasn't dodging the question, but no one was going to tell me how I should be. My life was my own.

Queerette:
It all ended so sadly.

Announcer:
In 1967, Bourbon had a car mishap and he needed to kennel the dogs that he was using in his act. He lodged them at a dog kennel, but when Rae couldn't pay the bill, the owner of the kennel sold the dogs for medical research.

Rae Bourbon:
(Somber, even teary eyed.)
He killed my dogs. That lowdown bastard killed them.

Queero:
Rae Bourbon had 70 dogs in the trailer.

Queerette:
For his act, all the dogs pissed on cue.

Queero:
Did I mention he had fallen on hard times?

Rae Bourbon:
I was going to pay that bastard. I wrote the governor and all the newspapers, but no one gave a damn. No one did a thing. Well, this fairy was not about to let that fly.

Queero:
Rae took matters into his own hands by hiring a couple thugs to go teach that man a lesson.

Announcer:
In Dec. 1968, the two young men drove Rae Bourbon's car to Texas. Intending to give the kennel owner a good thrashing, the beating went too far and the punks killed him.

Rae Bourbon:
It wasn't the worst news I ever heard, but I didn't want that to happen.

Announcer:
The two young men were found guilty of murder and Rae Bourbon was convicted of being an accomplice. Though 75 at the time, and in poor health, Bourbon was sentenced to 99 years in prison.

Queero:
The harsh sentence came after the judge looked over Boubon's arrest record with charges of indecency and immoral behavior.

Queerette:
That petty rap sheet so long you could wrap fish in it.

Gladys Bentley:
While in prison, Bourbon obtained a typewriter from his lawyer and started writing their memoirs.

Rae Bourbon:
I had plenty of stories to tell from my vaudeville days and plenty of other career highs and lows. Mine was the book every vaudevillian has inside them, with a little bit more.

Gladys Bentley:
There's no story like a backstage story.

Announcer:
Unfortunately Rae Bourbon's memoirs were not published. Bourbon wrote 300 pages worth of tales before dying of leukemia at age 78.

Rae Bourbon:
I hoped those memoirs might be another piece of my legacy, though I had no idea who might publish it. The how wasn't about to stop me. I had sold my music under the counter with my UTC label and I would have sold that story under the counter too if I had to.

Queero:
But death intervened.

Announcer:
And now Rae Bourbon performing The Chiropractor's Wife.

(Rae Bourbon performs)

Jean Marin:
Hollywood didn't know what to do with us queens, but then the Hays office stepped in and told them what to do with us — nothing. The Hays office named us No-No Number 4 on the 1930 Hollywood production code.

Rae Bourbon:
The pansies were whom they meant when they vowed to banish from the screen "any inference of sex perversion."

Gladys Bentley:
Bull daggers too.

Queerette:
Taboo I can tolerate.

Queero:
Taboo is enticing.

Gladys Bentley:
But they wanted to make the fairies and bull daggers disappear.

Queerette:
Unfit to be seen and heard.

Queero:
But we refused to vanish.

Queerette:
Slipping by the censors as fussy clerks and flustered waiters . . .

Queerette:
Paging Franklin Pangborn.

Queero:
We developed a queer code to get around the production codes.

Announcer:
Other rules from the Hays Office included: No pointed profanity; including the words God, Lord, Jesus, and Christ, unless they are used reverently in connection with proper religious ceremonies.

Gladys:
No licentious or suggestive nudity—in fact or in silhouette; and any lecherous or licentious notice thereof by other characters in the picture.

Queerette:
Don't you just love a big juicy mouthful of lawyer?

Queero:
I'd like to consult my counsel's briefs.

Gladys Bentley:
The Hays Office prohibited the depiction of the illegal traffic in drugs. No white slavery. No sexual relationships between races.

Announcer:
No talk of sexual hygiene or venereal diseases. No scenes of actual childbirth, and no "open" ridicule of races.

Queero:
"Open" is the operative word here.

Gladys Bentley:
Amen.

Announcer:
The final rule on the Production Code list was no children's sex organs, and no ridicule of the clergy.

Queero:
Interesting how the mention of children's sex organs made led them to no ridicule of the clergy.

Queerette:
And we were considered the menace.

Announcer:
Other pansies wish to be here this evening, but have other engagements. Sending his well wishes for the Pansies on Parade is Lester LaMonte aka Lestra LaMonte and his/her paper gowns.

Queerette:
Chic and crafty.

Announcer:
Our final pansy, Karyl Norman, was born in Baltimore in 1897. Like many of his fellow pansies, Karyl Norman was a vaudeville veteran by the age of 20.

Karyl Norman:
It took my a while to settle on a name. I took the stage name Karyl, because it was genderless, and Norman after my father. In New York, Karyl Norman was billed as "The Creole Fashion Plate" and gained notoriety for his gorgeous gowns.

Queero:
The handiwork of his mother who travelled with him.

Karyl Norman:
We were a team, mother and me.

Queero:
Norman and Mother this sounds familiar.

Gladys Bentley:
Back up. I have a question about being the Creole Fashion plate. How does that work?

Karyl Norman:
The booking agent gave it to me straight, he said it was less threatening to have an exotic Creole fantasy on stage than some white guy from Baltimore. I never darkened my skin or used cork. No blackface. My Italian roots proved exotic enough. I was born George Peduzzi.

Announcer:
Karyl Norman was the greatest mystery of them all. Norman left audiences to decide if they were male or female. Confirmation was not given regarding Norman's gender.

Karyl Norman:
I was billed as "Puzzling and Delightful" and "A Master Illusionist!"

Queero:
It was different.

Queerette:
Yes. Most pansies were anything but mysterious. You knew everything about them two minutes after you meet them.

Karyl Norman:
It wasn't just my love of fashion, my cross-dressing that led to the confusion.

Announcer:
Karyl Norman was born with an amazing gift, an unusual gift . . .

Karyl Norman:
I have an enormous . . .
(Queero and Queerette lean in)
Vocal range.

Queerette:
One reviewer crowed, "He or she... possesses equally good soprano and bass voices. Seldom does a woman show more grace, and seldom is a man more muscular."

Queero:
Karyl Norman was a sensation. The wardrobe dazzled theatregoers. He twirled about the stage in satins, silks, and marabou feathers.

Announcer:
Not only was Karyl Norman a great singer, they also wrote many of their own tunes, including "Nobody Lied (When They Said That I Cried Over You)", "Manzanilla", and "I'm Through (Shedding Tears Over You)".

Queero:
Karyl Norman's vaudeville show was full of witty repartee and songs with such ribald lyrics that audience members blushed.

Queerette:
The mother did not seem to mind.

Queero:
I heard she was the stage mother to end all stage mothers.

Queerette:
Mother and Norman were a team. Devoted to one another.

Queero:
Inseparable.

Announcer:
Karyl Norman toured the world. Back in New York they starred in the Greenwich Village Follies of 1924. In 1930 at the beginning of the Pansy Craze, Norman headlined at the Palace Theatre with Jean Malin in an act called "Glorifying the American Boy-Girl".

Malin:
We were a sensation.

Queero:
People loved Norman's impersonations. His Theda Bara . . .

Karyl Norman:
And I did not do impersonation. I did character impressions.

Queerette:
Well, Karyl Norman's top diva "character impression" during the Pansy Craze, was none other than a caricature of Joan Crawford in Rain.

Queero:
Joan heard about it and came to see for herself.

Karyl Norman:
I was shaking the night that Crawford came to see me. She and her pal, the actor Billy Haines, were seated dead center in the front.

Queero:
Miss Haines loved a good time.

Karyl Norman:
So did Crawford.

Queerette:
At least before she fancied herself queen of the manor.

Karyl Norman:
Miss Crawford came backstage after the show and gave me her stamp of approval.

Queero:
If Crawford had not approved, his career might well have been over.

Karyl Norman:
Thank goodness she understood that my impression was a tribute. Having Miss Joan Crawford attend the performance proved to be good publicity for us both.

Queero:
And Joan loved her publicity.

Queerette:
It's hypocritical that despite all the openness about fairies and queers, it was still a criminal offense.

Queero:
A sanitarium offense if things went bad.

Queerette.
Maybe jail.

Karyl Norman:
We walked a fine line.

Rae Bourbon:
That could snap at any moment.

Malin:
And we didn't have a net.

Karyl Norman:
Raids happened.

Bert Savoy:
They came with the territory.

Announcer:
With his two pianos and his mother's gorgeous gowns. Karyl Norman may have been the classiest of the pansies.

(Indignant sounds from the other performers in the dressing room.)

Announcer:
And now, Karyl Norman singing their hit recording, "Nobody Lied (When They Said That I Cried Over You)"

(Norman performs)

Announcer:
By the mid 1930s, Karyl Norman's popularity had diminished, but they continued to work in clubs. They went to Finocchio in San Francisco in 1937. Then later to Detroit to manage a place as well as perform.

Karyl Norman:
I spent years playing to all the gin and Judys, and I loved it.

Gladys Bentley:
That's what you do when show biz is all you know.

Malin:
Not in my blood, it was my blood.

Queero:
Or was it? Norman retired after their mother's death.

Karyl Norman:
There was no pleasure in it after mother died.

Announcer:
He lost the will to live. Karyl Norman died in 1947 at age 50 in Hollywood, Florida where he had recently appeared at the Ha Ha Club.

Queero:
Death really does have the last laugh.

Queerette:
We pansies had our own theater, our own social rules, our own culture, and even our own language.

Malin:
If I am playing checkers where would I be?

Rae Bourbon:
In a theater.

Queerette:
Playing checkers is moving seat to seat in a darkened movie theater in search of interested sex partners.

Queero:
I spent the afternoon playing checkers while Norma Shearer fled a lover on the Riviera.

Bert Savoy:
And what if they called me a muzzler.

Queero:
I'd say they were just being accurate.

Queerette:
A muzzler is a pansy who services a man orally.

Rae Bourbon:
And a gonsil is the receptive partner in anal sex and a jocker is the active partner.

Malin:
And when you are an out and very successful pansy, there are plenty of jockers to be had.

Rae Bourbon:
Every jocker has a price tag.

Bert Savoy:
I called them all bisexuals. Whenever I buy them something, they get sexual.

Queero:
Pure vaudeville.

Queerette:
How about basketeering.

Queero:
That's the visual appraisal of a man's crotch.

Queerette:
Seeing the sights as it were.

Queero:
And I've noticed several very talented audience members with us this evening.

Malin:
The ladies had stage door johnnies — and we had backstage willies.

Queerette:
In more ways than one.

Bert Savoy:
Trade and seafood galore.

Rae Bourbon:
When the wolves howled, we answered.

Announcer:
Bothwell Brown got them to howl for him when he was still on stage. As a performer, Bothwell Brown should have been bigger, but audiences and theater managers found his act seductive and unsettling.

Queerette:
Bothwell Brown went too far.

Queero:
He was a raid waiting to happen.

Bothwell Brown:
My audiences seemed to enjoy it. I had talent, big talent. Mack Sennett cast me as a cross-dressing aviator in his picture Yankee Doodle. Mack Sennett was the hottest thing in movies. Him casting me has to count for something. My career was doing just fine.

Malin:
All our careers were doing just fine.

Rae Bourbon:
The audiences weren't the ones who rejected us.

Malin:
The Pansy Craze didn't end.

Queerette:
It was halted.

Gladys Bentley:
They hate when it is not about them.

Queero:
Masculine Women and feminine men. Who is the rooster? Who is the hen?

Bothwell Brown:
Overnight we were on the butt end of a lot of phony outrage.

Malin:
And the Pansy Craze ended in 1933

Queero:
But all this just went underground.

Queerette:
If the mood is right and you dim the lights.

Queero:
Breath and hear.

Gladys Bentley:
The click of the needle, the buzz of the mic.

Bothwell Brown:
You hear the scratch, and the sudden jazz, and we are where we belong.

Announcer:
And now, the embodiment of "Hot Harlem", Gladys Bentley singing a number called Red Beans and Rice.

(Bentley performs.)

Announcer;
Thank you everyone. You've been a wonderful audience.

Queero:
(To audience)
The show is at an end.

Queerette:
(To audience)
But before you go remember — tipping isn't just for cows.

Gladys Bentley:
We would like to leave you with a song.

ENTIRE CAST JOINS IN SINGING Paper Moon:
(Breaking down stanzas for different duos/solos/etc.)

I never feel a thing is real
When I'm away from you
Out of your embrace
The world's a temporary parking place
A bubble for a minute
You smile, the bubble has a rainbow in it

Say, it's only a paper moon
Sailing over a cardboard sea
But it wouldn't be make-believe
If you believed in me

Yes, it's only a canvas sky
Hanging over a muslin tree
But it wouldn't be make-believe
If you believed in me

Without your love
It's a honky-tonk parade
Without your love
It's a melody played in a penny arcade

It's a Barnum and Bailey world
Just as phony as it can be
But it wouldn't be make-believe
If you believed in me

Yes, it's only a canvas sky
Hanging over a muslin tree
But it wouldn't be make-believe
If you believed in me

Without your love
It's a honky-tonk parade
Without your love
It's a melody played in a penny arcade

It's a Barnum and Bailey world
Just as phony as it can be
But it wouldn't be make-believe
If you believed in me

Songwriters: Billy Rose / E. Y. Harburg / Harold Arlen
(It's Only A) Paper Moon lyrics © Warner Chappell Music, Inc, S.A. Music, 1932.

Presenting
Wanda Lust

Cast

Wanda Lust

Narrator

Rick

Mick

Mike

Buck – Front desk attendant

Set

In the center of the stage is a smaller stage. This is where Wanda Lust stands and performs.

To the side of the stage is a mock set up of front desk at bathhouse. This is where Buck sits.

In the area in front of the stage are thrown pillows, etc. This is where Rick, Mick, and Mike recline at a social distance of six feet from one another while still facing the audience.

The narrator stands at a podium beside the onstage stage or can be offstage as well.

Presenting Wanda Lust

(As the scene opens Rick, Mick, and Mike are checking in at the front desk of a bathhouse. Buck, the attendant, has them sign a card and then gives them their locker key and a towel. One by one the men enter, strip down to just the towel, and lounge beside the stage.)
(The lights dim.)

Narrator:
Ladies and gentleman, tonight we welcome you to sit back, relax, and enjoy this hybrid of myth and history, memory and imagination — the sharing of a legend. Without further ado, we present — Miss Wanda Lust.
(A spotlight shines upon Wanda Lust as she takes the stage and lip synchs to Maggie Bell's 'Queen of the Night.')

Wanda:
Thank you. My name is Wanda Lust and I am a Virgo from Indianapolis.

Rick:
Indiana no-place was what she called it.

Wanda:
No offense Indianapolis, but I never fit in there. Nope became my mantra growing up there. Everywhere I looked I just found myself saying, nope. I'd rather not.

Rick:
Wanda felt destined for something more.

Wanda:
Or at least something else. I was born Stephen Jones. My birth name sounded like an alias. It was way too drab and forgettable.

Mike:
And those were two things Wanda never was.

Rick:
Even as a child.

Wanda.
I always told people my parents had three children, one of each.

(Buck does a bu-dum-bum hand roll on the entrance desk at the joke's punch line.)

Wanda:
(Stares at Buck and then to the audience.)
The help here can get fussy at times. I was about to say I was raised in a home that stressed modesty and humility. Neither of those appealed to me.

Mick:
You could say she rebelled.

Wanda:
But that was inaccurate. I escaped.

Rick:
She developed a vivid imagination.

Wanda:
I believed that as a baby I was kidnapped by Christians and that my real parents were great musicians.

Mike:
Not rock and rollers mind you,

Mick:
Or country or cabaret stars.

Rick:
Not Judy or Elvis or Billie or Patsy or even Peggy Lee.

Wanda.
I imagined my parents as great classical musicians.

Mike:
Wanda was a classical music aficionado, a child prodigy.

Wanda:
Owing to my Christian circumstances, I became a pipe organ tuner in Indianapolis.

Mike:
Servicing organs.

Wanda:
(To Mike)
I would say that was clever of you, but I try and be honest. While I was going around servicing organs . . .
(Looks to Mike awaiting wisecrack. Instead Mike shrugs.)
I realized I was not Stephen Jones from Indianapolis, not really.

Narrator:
As a fan of classical organ music, Wanda chose her drag name in honor of the famous classical organist, Wanda Landowska.

Rick:
And where did you get the Lust from?

Wanda:
Anywhere I could get it.

Buck:
(Does the ba-rum-pum roll again.)
The coroner declared that joke dead about 40 years ago.

Wanda:
My surname came from wanderlust. I was born with an adventurous soul and lusty heart. I was looking for a bigger world outside of Indiana.

Mike:
But in the meantime . . .

Wanda:
I began doing drag at the Famous Door on North Capitol Street in Indianapolis where guests were required to wear a coat and tie.

Mick:
The window dressing of respectability.

Narrator:
At the Famous Door, Wanda met Roby Landers who performed there with her Boylesque Review.

Rick:
Featuring "Some of the World's Most Famous Female Impersonators."

Narrator:
Meeting Roby Landers had a huge impact on Wanda. She saw Roby's work, Roby's dedication to her craft.

Wanda:
Roby had been in the business a decade by then, and she took her role as entertainer very seriously. She recognized talent. Roby helped bring me to Chicago where there were more opportunities.

Narrator:
In 1970, Indiana bars were dark on Sundays. Chicago offered not only more work, but more excitement as well.

Wanda:
And less Indiana.

Narrator:
In early 1971, Chuck Renslow opened Sparrows, a drag bar at 5224 N. Sheridan. Renslow named the place Sparrows to piss off queer writer Samuel Steward whose tattoo artist name was Phil Sparrow. Steward had done some underhanded things to Chuck after Renslow had spurned his affections. Chuck named his drag bar Sparrows because Steward loathed drag.

Rick:
I went to Sparrows from the start, even before Roby took over, back when Tillie the Dirty Old lady organized the shows there.

Mick:
Eventually that role went to Roby Landers, who had more experience as a stage manager and a deeper regard for the integrity of the show. Tillie was looking more for a good time.

Narrator:
At Sparrows, Roby organized the Roby Landers Hot Pants Revue and when she did, she asked her pal from Indianapolis, Wanda Lust, to join the show.

Wanda:
I had been saving up to move, and then this happened. I was going to make a name for myself in Chicago. I was ready for this. Give me a stage, give me an audience, and I'll make sure people know my name.

Rick:
We didn't have a choice.

Mick:
Wanda was larger than life from the start.

Mike:
And she looked it too. With her lean 6'3" frame, Wanda looked sensational in slinky outfits and was quite an outré dresser.

Mick:
In drag, Wanda was considered very pretty.

Rick:
Are you being shady?

Mick:
No, I was just making a comparison. Out of drag, Wanda was what you might call homely, with a long face and problem skin.

Wanda:
Well then lucky for you in all our encounters you were face down in a pillow.

Mike:
Ouch.

Mick:
In more ways than one. Wanda was hung like a horse.

Wanda:
That was part of my mystique. They called it my magic Wanda.

Mick:
Just one of the things that made Wanda, Wanda.

Wanda:
What made me feel full on Wanda was the make-up. I put it on thick to make my outsides match my insides. When that happened, it was magic.

Narrator:
Wanda was quoted as saying you need to get rid of your old face to put on a new one.

Mike:
The love for Wanda in Chicago came quickly.

Rick:
She was a standout.

Mick:
Avante-drag

Rick:
That's not a thing.

Mick:
No, but that was Wanda.

Narrator:
People began noticing, and they wanted to know more. In 1972, Wanda was interviewed by the Paper.

Wanda:
I've always enjoyed being a man. I don't think of myself as a woman trapped in a man's body. Actually, I think of myself as a male actress.

Narrator:
Wanda was not conflicted over who she was. She firmly believed that all people are a composite of an active male energy and a passive female energy.

Wanda:
My spiritual goal was always to develop, as best I could, both the male and the female energies inside me.

Mick:
She played male and female roles in the musical revues at Sparrows.

Rick:
Those shows at Sparrows that Roby Landers put together were sensational.

Mike:
Not just the revues. At Sparrows they also did surprise musicals too.

Rick:
South Pacific, Mame, Hair . . .

Mike:
And not all musicals. Once when I was there they did a parody of Erskine Caldwell's Tobacco Road.

Rick:
With Roby playing Ada in the production.
(Rick as Roby camping up the dialogue)
All you men is like that. There is a hundred more just like you all around here, and none of you is going to do nothing but talk.

Mick:
Pure camp..

Wanda:
In the musical parodies we used the music from the shows, but mostly our own dialogue.

Mick:
The format gave a quick queen like Wanda a place to shine, and that is precisely what she did.

Rick:
Those shows were a lot of fun at an affordable price.

Mike:
Even as a part time waiter I could afford to go.

Mick:
What else did you do?

Mike:
Whored around.

Buck:
Yep, he is in here every other night. Some weekends he even brings

luggage to Man's Country.

Mike:
I like to feel at home.

Buck:
Cozy as a crocheted sling.

Mick:
As I recall, I made you feel at home a couple times.

Wanda:
Excuse me. I am the bride at this wedding. Your story reminds me of an uncle of mine who we always had to remind to stay on topic.

Mike:
My point was, that a part time waiter and could afford the show at Sparrows. Admission was usually $2, which included two drink tickets, and I was always good at flirting for a drink or two more.

Wanda:
I brought the house down as the emcee in the Sparrows' production of Cabaret. It was double drag. I was a man in drag playing a man in drag.

Narrator:
At Sparrows, Wanda honed her skills at working a crowd. She had her signature songs.

Mike:
Her favorites included Linda Hopkins 'Deep in the Night,' and Irene Ryan's 'Just a Matter of Time' from the Broadway show 'Pippin.'

Rick:
Oh god yes, the Granny Clampett song.

Mick:
I remember Wanda performing a couple numbers from 'Let My People Come,' a big queer musical of the time.

Mike:
And Wanda milked each innuendo to perfection.

Narrator:
At Sparrows, Wanda got plenty of opportunity to shine behind the scenes as well. Her natural eye, her musical background, and her quick mastery of new skills proved invaluable when it came to working the sound and lights.

Wanda:
In no time I was better than the regular guy, but in his defense he was really stoned most of the time. I liked it here. Chicago was feeling like home. And getting laid was easy.

Rick:
Every night Wanda was bringing boys like me back to her place at Roscoe and Halsted.

Wanda:
Line up all you star fuckers, because I will be a star one day and you will be able to say, she fucked me way back when.

Narrator:
At the time, Wanda was living on the third floor of the building that currently houses The Chicago Diner, right next to the 7/11, which in Wanda's day was a Clark gas station.

Wanda:
I enjoyed working at Sparrows, but offers started coming in. And I wanted more - not just more money, but more fame. Brighter lights. My personality was too big not to be up in lights.

Mick:
For a while she joined the cast at the Baton.

Mike:
The line up there was superb; Dina Jacobs, Peaches, Jan Howard, Audrey Bryant, Lotta Love, Leslie Rejeanne, Roskie Fernandez, Felicia now and then, and

Wanda:
Me, of course.

Narrator:
At the Baton Wanda did individual numbers as well as group pieces, but there were no grand musicals that required her hilarious ad-libbing.

Rick:
Instead, Wanda Lust put those skills to use when she started to emcee the shows.

Mike:
Damn, she was funny, quick.

Wanda:
I was good at being an emcee, though I prefer to call it hostessing.

Buck:
Wanda knew how to work even the toughest crowd.

Rick:
No audience intimidated her.

Mick:
She could read a crowd and instinctively know how to control them.

Wanda:
What can I say? I'm a dominant top who likes attention.

Rick:
Hecklers beware!

Narrator:
Wanda was quick, and blessed with comic timing and delivery. One of her favorite intro lines to greet the crowd was . . .

Wanda:
Thanks for the clap, I've had everything else.

(Wanda looks to Buck.)

Buck:
I'm not going to do the punch line roll (ba-rum-dum) every single time you make a crack.

Narrator:
Wanda was a good dancer and could sing in her own bass voice as well.

Rick:
That voice — so booming and butch and unexpected.

Narrator:
She was called a tornado of talent.

Mick:
Wanda was also a performance art pioneer.

Rick:
Sometimes she did a sexy number

Mick:
And sometimes Wanda went for laughs.

Narrator:
Once at the Baton she lip synched to an instructional recording of 'How to Use an Appalachian Dulcimer.'

Mike:
That's right, an instructional recording on playing a regional

instrument.

Rick:
Way ahead of her time.

Wanda:
I got into some trouble at the Baton.

Mike:
There were issues.

Wanda:
Following rules was never a part of my skill set. I was disciplined about my performance and entertaining the crowd — but the rest was secondary to me. My "boyfriend" of the month, Christopher, and I liked to cook in my dressing room at the Baton, which was very much against the rules.

Mike:
The rules were easy — show up on time, no drugs, no sex on the premises, and no cooking in the dressing rooms.

Wanda:
Actually all of those were an issue for me at one time or another.

Narrator:
As a rule breaker, Wanda was frequently at odds with the stage director at the Baton, Roskie Fernandez. Often described as a taskmaster, Fernandez was frequently incensed by Wanda's casual disregard for the rules.

Wanda:
I hated conflict, so I left. The time was right for a change. A new place was opening further north that was looking for talent, . . . and they were willing to pay to get it.

Narrator:
In November of 1972, Wanda and several other Baton performers, moved to David's Place, a new drag venue at 5232 N. Sheridan.

Rick:
David's Place was laid out with two rooms, a bar and then a showroom with a proscenium arch stage where the cast did their numbers.

Mike:
What is a proscenium arch?

Rick:
(To audience)
The queens today are not what they used to me.
(To Mike)
Just think of it as a picture frame darling.

Wanda:
At David's Place we did musical parodies as well, like My Fair Laddie.

Mike:
The place was top notch in many ways.

Mick:
But the owners ruffled some feathers by coming in and thinking they were going to put everyone out of business. Not a way to make friends. They stole acts from other venues.

Wanda:
I wasn't stolen. I was bought.

Narrator:
David's Place was touted as having "Chicago's Most Unique Entertainment."

Mike:
Unique entertainment was another code phrase.

Wanda:
The David's cast while I was there was wonderful — Dina Jacobs, Audrey Bryant, Kiki St. John, Little Izzy.

Rick:
Little Izzy was a little person drag queen.

Wanda:
And there was Ebony Carr, Artesia Wells, and Taisha Wallace.

Mick:
Taisha did the costumes for all the group numbers as well.

Mike:
By the time she moved to David's, Wanda's emcee and hostess skills had made Wanda a hot commodity in town.

Wanda:
I was riding a wave. Gigs were rolling in.

Mick:
After two and a half years, Wanda was on her way to becoming the toast of gay Chicago.

Wanda:
By then I knew half the queers in town.

Buck:
But we all knew her.

Mick:
Wanda was hilarious, creative, eccentric, and wildly entertaining.

Rick:
Wanda's life was a performance.

Mick:
Or at least an ongoing event.

Mike:
It was not unusual to see Wanda on Clark Street wearing a hoop skirt, a cowgirl outfit, or a beaded gown trying to hail a cab to get to work or some benefit.

Narrator:
In an interview at the time, Wanda described herself as very organized, and very social.

Wanda:
"I'm trying to entertain people by being Wanda Lust, but Wanda is a public character, which allows me to be a private one too."

Rick:
Wanda hoped that she was entertaining as well as opening people's minds.

Wanda:
"I want to use drag to educate as well as entertain."
(To audience.)
Can you tell I used to watch a lot of beauty pageants? Just wait until you see my wave.
(More seriously)
I meant it, though. I did want to use my act to educate people. You can't get to know people through ignorance, but you can through laughter.

Narrator:
When the Man's Country Music Hall opened in April 1974, Wanda got her highest profile gig to date when the owner of the iconic bathhouse, Chuck Renslow, named Wanda as entertainment director.

Wanda:
I worked for Chuck at Sparrows. He knew I could entertain, manage a show, do sound, DJ, and even run the lights. By hiring me was saving a bundle. Chuck respected me. He knew I had a vision of how things should be, and that was important to him.

Rick:
Man's Country was more than a bathhouse. It was a pleasure and entertainment complex modeled after the Continental Baths in New York.

Mike:
Man's Country was about more than getting off.

Buck:
Man's Country was an experience.

Wanda:
My position was a queer creative control freak's dream job. Coordinating lights and sound, spinning records, handling talent, and entertaining.

Mick:
The job was ideal for her. Wanda knew how to keep a party going.

Rick:
Wanda brought innovation to the role.

Mike:
With Wanda running the show there were all sorts of surprises.

Mick:
As resident DJ, Wanda did not simply play records. She dictated the vibe.

Mike:
Every set was an expression.

Rick:
Her musical genius flourished as well as her eye for staging.

Buck:
Lots of compliments, and no complaints, at least not about the show.

Narrator:
Wanda exposed bathhouse patrons to new sounds and audio techniques. Wanda had a unique way of juxtaposing sounds and mixing styles.

Wanda:
The light and sound booth was a laboratory.

Narrator:
Soon Man's Country became known for classical music night mixes with an accompanying light show.

Mike:
It was stunning, and the last thing you would expect.

Rick:
I passed out in the Music Hall one night on a pile of pillows and woke up and Wanda was playing the 1812 Overture complete with the flashes and strobes. People were walking around dumbfounded.

Mick:
Wanda was the drug you took when you stepped foot into that enormous room.

Mike:
She mixed classical and heavy metal.

Mick:
And porn music with porn "sounds" in an extended remix while playing porn on three enormous screens around the room. Two minutes and everyone in the music hall started getting it on.

Rick:
We gave ourselves over to her vision.

Mick:
And if Wanda didn't like what was playing when it was her turn to spin — she would drag the needle across the record and announce in her booming bass voice.

Wanda:
The music is changing, NOW.

Narrator:
In a 1974 Chicago Tribune piece, comic and writer Bruce Vilanch called Mans Country: the Hottest Spa in Town and spoke specifically of Wanda as, "a 6'4" drag queen with a rapier wit, sensational figure, and more red hair than Rhonda Fleming.

Wanda:
I was working so much at Man's Country that my apartment on Roscoe and Halsted went unused. I lived mostly in loungewear in a room on the second floor of the bathhouse.

Rick:
She was always there, surrounded by her flock of young gays.

Mike:
They worshipped her.

Mick:
She was a living legend. She even went as some kid's date to a high school prom.

Wanda:
Guilty as charged. That prom was in the southwest suburbs, not exactly my usual crowd, but I went. You can't avoid something just because it scares you. I stayed long enough to make it clear that I was the best dressed of the evening.

Narrator:
As entertainment director at Man's Country, Wanda always made the visiting performers feel at home.

Wanda:
I did everything in my power to guarantee a guest star's success. I may have played and partied, but I took my duties very seriously.

Buck:
All sorts of acts appeared at Man's Country and they all adored her: comics, singers, bands, magicians, and hypnotists. Man's Country was a top stop on the K-Y Circuit.

Mike:
That's what insiders called the tour route for performers working the gay bar and bathhouse venues.

Buck:
Man's Country was a big deal and I was always proud to say I worked here.

Narrator:
When film and burlesque star Sally Rand came to Man's Country to perform her balloon dance, Wanda applied Sally's body paint, did her lights, did her music, and even tended to Sally's big balloon and her feathered hand fans.

Wanda:
Sally liked how I painted her curves and crevices. She asked me to go on the road with her as her manager and opening act, even do her lights and costumes. I was tempted. The pay was good. I never got the chance to say either way. Shortly after she asked me, Sally got ill, and the final tour she planned never happened.

Rick:
We were relieved to hear Wanda was staying. Man's Country would not have been the same without her.

Buck:
Wanda was the heart and soul of the place.

Narrator:
In 1976, Wanda was the centerpiece atop the Man's Country bicentennial Pride Parade float.

Buck:
Atop a sea of red, white, and blue, there was Wanda, as Lady Liberty herself.

Mick:
In a pointed red bra, flaming hair piled on her head, and wearing the flag as a sort of sarong.

Nick:
Old Glory never had it so good.

Buck:
And instead of a torch in this Lady Liberty's upraised arm, Wanda held…

Wanda:
A really big dildo.

Mick:
The crowd on the curb went wild when they saw her.

Rick:
I know I did.

Mike:
Wanda loved making people look.

Mick:
And listen.

Rick:
And especially laugh.

Mick:
Wanda was a big old prankster.

Wanda:
Guilty as charged.

Rick:
For New Year's Eve 1977, Wanda asked Mr. Man's Country if he would be a human disco ball.

Wanda:
He wanted to be a star so, naturally, he obliged.

Buck:
To transform him into a disco ball, Wanda glued little pieces of mirror all over his body and had him stand on a giant turntable that had been specially constructed for the New Year's celebration.

Wanda:
As the human disco ball, he was going to stand on the turntable and revolve for a song at midnight.

Buck:
Unfortunately for Mr. Man's Country, Wanda loved to remix music almost as much as she practical jokes.

Mike:
By the time she was finished, the two-minute song she had originally asked him to spin with was over fifteen minutes.

Mike:
I have to give him credit — Mr. Man's Country did stay on that turntable the entire time.

Buck:
And we just watched him go around

Mick:
And around.

Mike:
And around.

Rick:
When the song eventually stopped he took a bow and stumbled into a wall.

Mike:
I would have pissed my pants, but all I was wearing was a towel.

Mick:
Wanda was full of stories.

Buck:
Like the story of Wanda's blue fox cape and how it once belonged to ice-skating champion and film star Sonja Henie.

Narrator:
After her film career ended, Sonja Henie toured the country for years with her Hollywood Ice Productions. Eventually, the ice show folded. At the time, Henie was living in Evanston with her husband. When she died in 1969 her old ice show outfits ended up in storage at a costume warehouse on the corner of Drummond and Clark in Lincoln Park. Eventually, the warehouse needed space. To clear out some stock, they had a fire sale on gowns, circus outfits, and assorted costumes, including those from Henie's ice show.

Wanda:
Once word got out every queen in town showed up. The place was a madhouse. Sequins and feathers and rhinestones everywhere. Most of those bedazzled outfits were going for $5-$20. I'm about a foot taller than Sonja Henie, so not much of hers was going to fit me.

Rick:
Then Wanda looked across the room, and on the end of a rack she saw the blue fox cape.

Mick:
And she knew.

Wanda:
It spoke to me, and so did the two-level teardrop tiara and matching zirconium neckpiece I found a couple minutes later.

Narrator:
To celebrate her purchase of the cape and jewels, Wanda did an impromptu photo shoot on the hood, and eventually roof of a taxicab until the driver ran out of the diner and chased Wanda and her boyfriend away!

Mick:
The photo ran in Gay Life.

Rick:
Wanda was queer Chicago's It Girl.

Mike:
At Chuck Renslow's annual White Party, the event of the queer social season. Wanda made her grand entrance descending the winding staircase of the Dewes Mansion in an enormous ante-bellum gown.

Rick:
Wanda was working that staircase and god help the person who set foot on those stairs before she had fully descended.

Mike:
Every stair seemed like a statement.

Mick:
Very lady of the manor.

Buck:
Wanda had earned that crowd's attention. Wanda had been through some shit. Hard times, harassment, hassles. Wanda's chipped front tooth came from having a brick thrown in her face on the street.

Wanda:
What was I going to do, go to the cops?

Mike:
Instead of being self-conscious about it, Wanda turned her chipped tooth into a joke.

Wanda:
I told folks it made it easier for me to snag a trick.

Mike:
Wanda was always around, always telling stories or making jokes. So we all noticed her absence when she went back home for a week.

Mick:
She left her drag and borrowed a friend's car.

Wanda:
My dad was sick.

Narrator:
Despite their history and differences, Wanda needed to be there.

Wanda:
We were not close. I never came out and told him I was gay. I just disappeared into my own gay life. When I went home before he died he told me that we just see the world differently. He said he knew what kind of person I was inside. He said that was what mattered.
(Pause. Wanda is teary.)

Narrator:
In the mid 1970s, a group of doctors began STD testing at Man's Country. These young physicians were ushering in a new and judgment free approach to gay men's health.

Mick:
The gay men's health awareness movement was born from a need to diagnose and treat STDs.

Narrator:
Getting tested and treated for venereal disease was simply the responsible thing for sexually active gay men to do.

Rick:
A shot of penicillin now and again was a small price to pay for sexual liberation.

Buck:
The young doctors began a weekly program of testing here.

Narrator:
From that came the Chicago Gay Health Project, which opened a small permanent testing area upstairs at Man's Country.

Mick:
People would come in and get tested. No big deal.

Buck:
We even had people come in just to get tested.

Rick:
The goal was to dispel the stigma and shame of STDs.

Wanda:
Around this time my friend and Man's Country manager Gary Chichester was hospitalized with hepatitis. To cheer him up, I dressed up as a nurse and snuck into the hospital to visit him.

Rick:
And thus was born another part of the Wanda Lust legacy, her activism as Nurse Lust.

Wanda:
The first time I put on the nurse's uniform and the cap I knew exactly who Nurse Lust was, and who I was as her.

Mike:
Overnight Wanda became involved with the STD clinic at Man's Country.

Rick:
Some said she had a crush on one of the doctors.

Wanda:
Maybe at the very start.

Mick:
But Wanda's dedication was real. On the nights the clinic was open, you would always see her: white uniform, big black spectacles, her hair up in a bun, and white pumps.

Mike:
Wanda made the STD clinic a fun place to be. Getting tested there was a good time as well as the responsible thing to do.

Narrator:
As Nurse Lust, Wanda helped gay men embrace their sexual health. She appeared on posters promoting VD testing in a pose reminiscent of Uncle Sam recruitment poster.

Wanda:
(Assuming the pose.)
I Want YOU to Get Tested.

Rick:
And her hepatitis posters were yellow.

Mick:
Yellow eyes are the first sign of Hep B. That was the sickest I had ever been, at least until later.

Narrator:
In addition to the posters, Nurse Lust contributed to gay men's sexual health and awareness by accompanying the STD mobile testing unit.

Rick:
Also known as the VD van.

Buck:
The VD van made the rounds on weekends, parking on the street outside of popular queer clubs and nightlife areas.

Mick:
River North.

Mike:
Clark and Division

Rick:
Clark and Diversey.

Buck:
When the VD van pulled to the curb, Nurse Lust would leap from the vehicle and run into bars to try and get guys come to the van and get tested for STDs.

Rick:
Wanda had a clipboard so you knew she meant business.

Mike:
And if you went with Nurse Lust to get tested, she gave you a cookie.

Mick:
I got a cookie.

Mike:
We all did.

Mick:
Mine had icing.

Wanda:
I liked giving out my cookies.

Narrator:
And Wanda's methods got results. Wanda Lust and the VD bus rolled onto the streets of Chicago in the week of September 23 to September 29 of 1975, and in that first week over 1,000 people were tested for venereal diseases.

Mick:
Wanda had a way of making whatever she was doing the thing to do.

Buck:
She pushed it sometimes.

Narrator:
One evening in at Man's Country in 1977, a patron stayed in the steam room too long.

Buck:
I guess he came out of the steam room light headed, got dizzy, fell into the whirlpool, and drown.

Mike:
I was there that night, although I was otherwise occupied. I heard about it later in the snack bar.

Narrator:
The police were called.

Buck:
A last resort at any bathhouse.

Narrator:
The accident site was secured awaiting the arrival of the authorities.

Wanda:
The accident was horrible, and it was also spoiling everyone else's evening. I wanted folks to have fun. So I did something I should not have done.

Buck:
An understatement.

Wanda:
My heart really was in the right place.

Narrator:
Wanda intentionally tampered with a death scene prior to investigation, or even the appearance of the coroner, by floating a mannequin in the whirlpool.

Wanda:
We used a department store mannequin that we called "Ed" to put behind the snack counter as a joke when the attendant went on break. He was standing right there, fifty feet away. The prank was all but asking to be pulled.

Buck:
Wanda went behind the counter, took Ed, stripped him, and floated him face down in the whirlpool. The cops were pissed, but Chuck Renslow was madder.

Mike:
Nobody likes it when Daddy is mad.

Wanda:
Especially me. Chuck didn't fire me, but things were different. He put a lot of stock in obedience and I had defied that. Truthfully, if it hadn't been this it would have been something else. Things were good at Man's Country, but it was time for a change. I chose the name Wanda Lust for a reason.

Narrator:
Not long after the incident, the Club Baths in Kansas City announced they were looking for someone to do basically what Wanda had already been doing at Man's Country.

Wanda:
It was less money, but I didn't make decisions that way. It was new. It was an adventure. Besides, I could get more bang for my buck in Kansas City. The opportunity just opened like a door and sometimes when that happens you just know. And it turned out the manager at the Club Baths was Frank who I knew when he lived in Chicago and managed the Gold Coast.

Rick:
Frank had been in Kansas City a few years.

Wanda:
I called the number in the ad. We talked and Frank remembered me. After fifteen minutes on the phone he offered me the job, and I accepted it.

Mike:
And in the summer of 1978, Wanda Lust left Chicago.

Mick:
I don't think she was in the Pride Parade that year.

Mike:
If Wanda was within a mile of the parade, you knew.

Rick:
And like that, Wanda headed west.

(Action moves to the Club Baths in Kansas City, Buck gets up and carries the booth to the other side. Mick, Rick, and Mike rearrange the pillows and move into different positions. The narrator's podium remains stationary.)

(Wanda performs Linda Hopkins, 'Deep in the Night.')

Wanda:
Overnight I became the bathhouse diva at the Club Baths with a new town to conquer. Frank gave me free rein at the baths. The setup was a bit of a challenge. First thing I did was to have a mirror ball installed over the swimming pool.

Buck:
There was no stage at the Club Baths,

Wanda:
I didn't realize how good I had it with the Music Hall at Man's Country. But I am not one to look back. At Club Baths, most of my performances were done poolside. I only performed in the water, ala Esther Williams, a handful of times and ever time I ended up looking like a drowned rat.

Buck:
Even sopping wet Wanda had that something extra.

Mike:
Kansas City saw it too.

Mick:
Her outrageous performances and innovative music made her the talk of the town.

Wanda:
I moved in with Frank when I first arrived in town. Mostly I needed a place to house my music. Music was always my greatest pleasure and greatest indulgence. I had hundreds of albums, most of them classical.

Rick:
Technically, Wanda was living on the third floor of Frank's rented home, but, like she did at Man's Country, Wanda basically took up residence at the Club Baths.

Wanda:
I paid no rent, had sex at my disposal, and had a cleaning staff. Why

wouldn't I live at the bathhouse?

Mike:
I think she lived here because of all those things, but the main reason was that Wanda Lust loved nothing more than to hold court and by living there she always had an audience.

Mick:
Soon Kansas City queers had their own tales of Lust.

Buck:
One day a Great Dane escaped from it's owner outside the baths and ran inside, jumped the turnstile. It was crazy. The owner was frantic and did not know what to do. He was cute, but hesitant to enter. I told him to stick close.

Rick:
They found the dog in Wanda's room. Wanda had painted the dog's nails bright red and added a pink ribbon around each ear.

Buck:
The owner of the dog was thankful, but told Wanda that the dog was a male. Wanda looked the owner dead in the eye and said,

Wanda:
So, what's your point?

Buck:
Wanda was there when the Club Baths flooded with six inches of water.

Wanda:
I woke up in the middle of the flood and felt like I was working at Club Venice. The water downstairs was up to my knees, and I'm rather leggy.
(Shows leg.)
I've been told they're showgirl caliber.

Buck:
All this water was rushing in and none of us knew what to do. Kansas City didn't know what to do. These floods were historic.

Rick:
Wanda grabbed the widescreen TV from the break room and waded out the door and to a coffee shop up the street.

Wanda:
That flood really put a damper on things. I sat there with the TV and thinking that it was time for me to book an out of town gig or two.

Rick:
When she said things were getting a little too Biblical at the Club Baths. I assumed she was talking about the flood.

Buck:
Once the water receded, we just hosed out the mud. It may have been a historic flood, but this was a gay bathhouse. It was business as usual in less than 36 hours.

Mick:
As if nothing had happened.

Buck:
Another time the police were in pursuit and the suspect ran inside the Club Baths and hurdled the turnstile.

Rick:
I was getting ready to go inside when I saw the flashing blue lights in front and decided to do something else for a while.

Buck:
When the cops came in shouting and making demands, I told them they had to have memberships to get inside. Did I mention I am a bit of a smartass? So then the head cop blows his whistle and yells.

Mike:
Buzz us in or we'll kick the fucking doors down and round everyone up, including you, faggot.

Buck:
Man I hate cops.

Mike:
So two cops are running through the bathhouse kicking open doors, the whole bit, and they ended up outside the orgy room. Wanda was standing just outside the door, smoking a cigarette.

Wanda:
Not loitering so much as observing.

Rick:
The cops flashed their lights around the orgy room.

Mick:
But no one stopped doing anything.

Wanda:
I nodded towards the room. No dead bodies in there, officer. They all seem pretty lively. I thought the cop was going to punch me, especially after hearing someone giggle at my remark from the darkness.

Buck:
The way they ran in here, I thought the guy they were chasing killed someone. Turns out, the guy they were chasing was hustling.

Mike:
Somebody must have pulled him into a room.

Buck:
The cops left empty handed and kicked open the door on their way out.
(Out the door)
Good to see you again officers.

Narrator:
While working at Club Baths, Wanda put herself out there. With her charisma and wit she was soon hosting various gigs — bar nights, benefits, and fundraisers.

Rick:
She made a splash by coming to the Pride Parade dressed as Carrie White.

Wanda:
(as Carrie) "Breasts Mama. They're called breasts, and every woman has them."

Narrator:
In Kansas City, Wanda also resumed her work on behalf of gay men's sexual health awareness. Working with the Kansas City Health Department, Wanda started a mobile STD testing unit there.

Rick:
Fortunately she packed her nurse uniform.

Mike:
And like that, Nurse Lust was reborn.

Rick:
But she no longer drove a van. In Kansas City, the Nurse Lust mobile testing unit was a M*A*S*H* unit jeep.

Wanda:
Just call me Hot Lips.

Rick:
We already have.

Wanda:
My promise of a cookie was just as popular.

Narrator:
In October of 1979, Wanda was one of an estimated 100,00 who attended the huge rally, the National March on Washington for Lesbian and Gay Rights. Organizers of the event had demands: a comprehensive lesbian/gay rights bill passed in Congress, a presidential executive order banning discrimination based on sexual orientation, the repeal all anti-lesbian/gay laws, the end of discrimination in lesbian mother and gay father custody cases, and the protection of gay and lesbian youth from laws which are used to discriminate against or harass them in their homes, schools, jobs and social environments.

Wanda:
I believed in everything they were saying and I knew it was important to show up. Making our voices heard was important. Seeing that many of us — together — that was historic.

Narrator:
Having a deathly fear of flying, Wanda took the train to Washington D.C. instead.

Wanda:
The most glamorous means of travel, in the brochures anyway.

Narrator:
Wanda decided to extend her travels a bit and visited Chicago on her way home.

Mick:
At the time Wanda was sporting a full beard. On her face, not at her side.

Mike:
We still recognized her. She had that voice.

Rick:
And she was wearing the Nurse Lust t-shirt.

Buck:
Wanda dropped by Man's Country to say hello. I was working the desk that night and chatted a bit. Wanda was only in town a few days, then back to K.C. for another gig. She said she was happy and I could tell she meant it.

Narrator:
At the end of the week Wanda took the train to Kansas City for Steppin' Out, an extravaganza she was hosting. At the gala, Wanda performed while straddling a six-foot mylar moon hoisted 22 feet above the floor. Over 800 people were in attendance.

Mike:
One reporter covering the event for the Kansas City Star called Wanda, a totally outrageous and imposing comedienne whose risqué sense of humor appealed to gay and straight members of the audience. A composite of old Hollywood glamour mixed with a bit of Carol Burnett chutzpah.

Mick:
Lightning had struck twice.

Wanda:
That was nice, but I was ready for more.

Rick:
Hungry for more.

Mick:
She was Wanda Lust for a reason.

Wanda:
I had been keeping my ears open. Early in 1980, I got word that I was hired full time at a big queer discotheque in Houston.

Rick:
Miss Lust was starting the decade off right!

Mike:
Wanda started to let people know and made some goodbyes.

Buck:
Though Wanda didn't say goodbye, she always said, until we meet again.

Wanda:
I was planning to leave town at the end of February. I'd go down to Houston first and then come back to get the rest of my things from Frank later.

Narrator:
On Tuesday, February 19, 1980, Wanda decided to see the John Carpenter movie, the Fog, at the Empire Theater with her lover and a friend.

Wanda:
We went to my favorite spot, the middle section towards the front.

Narrator:
Seated behind them were a man and two women who were talking loudly throughout the movie. Several people tried to quiet them.

(Rick and then Mick and then Mike all turn around and shush.)

Narrator:
Finally, with about ten minutes left in the movie, Wanda turned around and in her deep booming voice bellowed,

Wanda:
Would you please shut the fuck up and watch the movie.

Narrator:
The trio gave Wanda a dirty look followed by a brief exchange of words.

Wanda:
We thought that was the end of it.

Mike:
After the lights came up, Wanda headed up the stairs to leave the theater by a side exit.

Rick:
The people she had shushed were directly in front of Wanda and her friends.

Mike:
Suddenly, the man turned around and said, "Motherfucker," before stabbing Wanda multiple times in the gut with a seven-inch blade.

Mick:
Wanda sank to her knees.

Mike:
And fell slowly onto her back.

Rick:
Her lover tried to stop the bleeding, but it was no use.

Wanda:
I can see his face, and his eyes, and then your face, and your eyes, and then . . .an audience of eyes and a spotlight and the muffled sounds of a crowd.

Narrator:
Wanda was dead in less than four minutes. She died bleeding on the sidewalk, cradled in her boyfriend's arms, waiting for the ambulance to arrive.

Rick:
Wanda was pronounced dead on the scene before being taken to Truman Medical Center.

Narrator:
The assailant fled through an alley northwest of the theater and was eventually picked up in Texas. He was returned to Kansas City and arraigned on capital murder charges, which were later dropped to second-degree murder. Eventually he was sentenced to ten years for Wanda's murder.

Mick:
Not sure how long he actually served?

Buck:
Maybe two or three.

Narrator:
The Empire Theater, where Wanda was stabbed that night, was shuttered for good in 1985.

Rick:
Wanda was cremated.

Mike:
The formal services all took place in Indiana and were announced as private. Meaning family.

Rick:
It was just as well. We knew Wanda Lust, but those services were for Stephen Jones.

Wanda:
And he died years ago.

Narrator:
Aside from her Father's deathbed acceptance, Wanda said her Presbyterian family had never been tolerant of her. According to Frank, the family went through Wanda's belongings and took her classical music collection, her coin collection, her costume jewelry, and even the blue fox cape that once belonged to Sonja Henie.

Mike:
Then came back for the wigs and gowns and everything but her shoes.

Narrator:
A second memorial for Wanda Lust was held two weeks later at Wellington Avenue United Church of Christ in Chicago.

Wanda:
The place was packed with friends and admirers.

Mike:
The mourners overflowed onto the sidewalk and street.

Wanda:
Although I had left town two years before, hundreds of queer Chicagoans gathered to pay their respects.

Mick:
We showed up to celebrate you and honor family.

Rick:
And to say thank you.

Wanda:
You're welcome, darling. Every bit of it was a labor of love. Until we meet again.

(Wanda blows a kiss, bows, and turns. As she walks away as the stage turns black.)

COVID Summer

Sidewalk Theater
Recorded
June-August 2020

Staging

Staging of COVID Summer is a simple doorway with a stool before it. The doorway looks out onto a busy street and sidewalk. Traffic noises may be included. Streams of people pass the doorway, some are wearing masks and some are not. The groupings are random, sometimes singles, sometimes in pairs, sometimes a pack. At points the dialogue is shouted, sometimes in a normal speaking voice, and some dialogue is being said into or out of a phone. Some passersby are silent. Some who pass just turn and stare into the doorway.

The observer on the stool is silent. When addressed directly by a passerby, they answer in a non-verbal manner: waving, nodding, or shaking their head yes or no.

Many lines spoken in this experiment were not recorded in this text simply because I don't know any other languages and didn't understand what was being said. Any production of this material is free to translate any of the below lines into any language of their choosing.

COVID Summer

Person at Door:
After the initial shut downs with COVID precautions in Illinois and Chicago, there was a gradual re-opening of the city. Part of my new duties was to sit at the doorway for hours.

When people entered I told them to keep their mask in place, try to maintain social distance, and that we preferred credit, debit, and Apple pay. I also had a tally counter to keep track of the number of patrons in the store. We had a limited capacity of 10. If more then 10 wished to enter the store, it was my job to handle the line outside and see that it formed properly.

The front door of the store opens directly on to Broadway in Lakeview. The owner of the store liked us to keep the door open for circulation as well as to let people know they could come in and browse. The area has very heavy sidewalk traffic — sometime during the weeks of sitting at the door I started to eavesdrop.

--Good morning (waves in the door)

--Jenny was fine. Joyce was not happy.

--I need to get in touch with that school.

--Do people even buy dictionaries anymore?

--It's three weeks away.

--There are two of them. (Holds up two fingers.). Two.

--Next to it used to be a French bakery.

--I hope to get the keys tomorrow.

--(In door) Do you have cribbage boards?

--So, I told you I'm back in school, right? I'm taking some English classes.

--I don't like to be there too long.

--You think you're so funny.

--It's been going on for a while and just progressively getting worse.

--They keep talking about it, but I haven't heard a thing.

--Will you hurry?

--It was a 55-minute trip to his house.

--Don't know how I bruised my hip the other day
    The train?
    Yeah

--This has happened twice in the past week, and it should not be happening.

--You closed the door on my foot.

--In that moment she was single.

--I can't even focus.

--Wait, what?
    Huh?
    I thought you said something.

--I don't think that should be an issue.

--Oh my gosh! How cute!

--How do you not weight 500 pounds living across from Stan's Donuts?

--Do you want me to wait for you?

--He's telling me about a bad connection.

--I'm down with doing whatever.

--That was our last shopping trip

--He needs to step up and the other one needs to get lost.

--I wish I could wait until January.

--He reached out to the recruiter again.

--You guys are leaving?

--They are smart videos.

--I'm so tired of this. Aren't you tired of this?

--You can't just tell him what you want to do?
  No

--It was rough. It was just really rough.

--You can't pick and choose. You're either all in or all out.

--A lot of it was overkill.

--I just don't care anymore

--The lake here in August is nice.

--Hi (looking in door.)

--Can I just finish my thought?

--It's a nice pocket, but the areas around it are pretty rough. They said I wouldn't have to deal with that, but I said bullshit.

--We can just have a good rest tonight.

--I don't know, Saturday?

--You've been in there. You've bought something in there.
   I know

--So, this is what's weird.

--(Looks in door) Hi. How has business been?

--Shut up! Tie your shoelace!

--Yeah, I had that too.

--Boy it's hot out today.

--Obviously that should have been done a long time ago.

--Should we do it at 1:00, 1:15, or 1:30?

--I haven't seen anyone in months.

--We can go back to the restaurant we went to when we were biking.

--You know how she is about pillows.

--How worried are you?

---Oh shit!
   What?
   Nevermind

--Have you done any yoga lately?

--Wait. Will you wait please?

--He needs to know he messed up.

--Oh my God! Where were you?
    I was there.

--She's a survivor.

--I didn't really binge watch it. I never watched more than 4 episodes at a time.

--Well, that's not your problem.

--He was carrying it.
    He was?

--Thank you. Thank you God for being a leader.

--This happened pre COVID.

--Do you have hand sanitizer?

--They were to scale.

--I love that place.
    Me too.

--Dude, play the game. Just tell me.

--You really shouldn't
    I know.

--She got on me about the math.

--They needed more, but they were just things.

--I didn't want to be there either.

--I practically live here.

--(In door) I am so glad you are open.

--He tells me every time I see him.

--You put in so much work just to make people laugh.

--The maid of honor just texted me.

--I'm in the mood for something new.
    Me too.

--That's so cool, what are you going to do?
    What can we do?

--You don't have to be Jewish to eat tater tots.

--Send me a picture.

--The air is so thick when it's like this.

--Are you open open?

--I want to be the bad boy of pilates.

--They usually do it, but they didn't today.

--I just went along with it.

--(In door) Do you allow children?

--I definitely want to stop and take a look.

--You are fine. It's just a cold. Carrie is fine. We are all fine.

--Anything is better than what you have.

--You need to realize there are people behind you.

--This is the first time I've worn sandals all summer.

--Wow.
   I know.
   Really?
   Yes.

--I don't want to keep doing this if it isn't getting better.

--There's no push to get it done.

--I don't care how much he begs, I am not doing that.

--This town smells like weed.

--Why? You don't have to be like this, Frank.

--I know exactly what I want to do.

--Do they ticket along here?

--You're good, Brother.

--The other day when you weren't here I got to-go food and brought it home.

--I've always been one of the first to get them.

--I'm good. You know me. I'm good.

--I was like; my friend will probably prefer it.

--What is the capability?

--Sarah, where did you get your hair done?

--It was a fucking cat!

--Part of me really wishes this would all work out.

--I realized later that I read the wrong book.

--Not everyone likes her.

--I am going to tell him we are coming because I don't want any surprises.

---It was a spider or something.

--So, we need a mask to come inside?

--I texted, so they can figure out the rest of it.

--I was there for a long time; I know the way it was.

--I like your mask.

--I finished most of it. Not all of it, but most of it.

--I'm a mom too you know.

--This is a bookstore

--There's never any shade around here.

--(In door.) Do you have that book by his niece?

--Were they indoors or outdoors? I am not going to do indoors.

--He said that?
   Yes.
   What did you say?
   What do you think?

--They don't have anything for me now.

--It's the street after this one, I think.

--(In door) What book is hot right now?

--Alex will do it. Eddie, on the other hand...

--What's going on with Don now?

--We waited. Not that it mattered.

--I've got a baby!

--There are enough people to keep a list.

--(Looking in.) Is it okay? Is it okay?

--I like that, I think.

--If I had the money I would be out of there. You know that.

--Is this a store?

--We need more people during peak times.

--They became a couple because of quarantine.

--He's the one who did all the work for me.

--Can you keep an eye on my bike?

--Are you open?

--That's a great mask.

--That's a good book.
  I know. I recommended it to you.

--(In door) So what is your job? Nevermind.

--In my mind I thought, No.

--They told us to keep to ourselves.

--Is this, like, a real bookstore?

--Just take a selfie like a normal person!

--He wasted about 6 trillion dollars. Six trillion!

--That only happens when I black out.

--Of course he meant it. He posted it.

--I'm trying to get something set up.

--Things seem healthy.

--I'm just going to lay low. I'm like, scared of everything.

--Where have you been?

--Is there anything that you would like?

--The situation you described was not that.

--I think he has 150 and we're at 95 now.

--It's not really work — it's a zoom meeting.

--I don't want to be defiant or anything, but no.

--The friend who was letting us stay there started chiming in.

--You can't just walk into stores.

--Oh shut up! No he doesn't.

--That is a scandal.

--I've started taking antihistamines.

--So she got upset.

--I had one last night.

--Are you okay with it, or are you not?

--That is their disease.

--I think 35 is best.

--Like the email said, I didn't realize how good I had it.

--What are those bike things called?
　Divvy?

--Whenever I see her she pretends she doesn't see me.

--I use a surgical mask.

--Examples were collected from the different tech supports.

--We spent hours just sitting there.

--He did that and then just sent me on my way.

--I am always the last one to know.

--It is still my business.

--She posted a picture.

--The spacing was different depending on how you looked at it.

--Don't whine, that never helps, ever.

--That's where all the money went.

--There are long-term effects as well.

--Isn't there a card store along here?

--He said 1:00 originally. I got here at 5 minutes early and I got a text that said it would be 1:30 so I don't know what I'm going to do.

--I don't care what she does.
    The sister?
    Yes

--I don't recall ever seeing or speaking to them

--That shouldn't be news. Why is that news?

--It's growing out of the ground.

--He has not returned my text or my call.

--They post about everything else. I don't know why this is special.

--Just allergies, not corona. Nobody freak out.

--That happened in the day world.

--Until you know for sure, don't do it.

--Our windows stick. Can we get new windows?

--I need to watch that again.

--She's going to stop working for them soon.

--No
   Yes.
   Seriously?

--We've been hanging out together.

--When that happened I was like, well this is fucking stupid.

--Did you ever think for a second that maybe they don't want to?

--I am so hot.

--I want to say probably, but I'm not sure.

--I was just being honest.

--That car was 5500 bucks.

--It would come up behind me and snarl.

--I don't think they can do it tomorrow.

--They were new people so I was like, Oh God.

--They want you to take a shower. They want you to get ready.

--In some ways it wasn't your fault.

--Tomorrow should be better.

--I don't think my mom is going to like that.

--If you're the only one, you have to come get it.

--You need to see season one for it to make sense.

--I am not going to say a word until the rug goes down.

--I have that with pizza.

--I was confused before, but now it totally makes sense.

--I don't care what we do as long as we do something.

--They were eating right behind you.

--I freaked out. Not a single patient was doing it.

--Let me grab a coffee first.

--He was managing and guiding the team.

--The whole thing messed with my head.

--You're lagging behind.

--There was some grumbling, but for the most part they were okay.

--I wanted to go there for a while, but I kept forgetting about it.

--Versus thirty minutes there and back.

--I wasn't a fan to begin with.

--At least there were options.

--It's entirely that way — it's always been entirely that way.

--I want to hug you.

--Alex texted me, again.

--Do you remember that one candle we had?

--So, technically, you're on my side.

--At least I haven't heard about cross fit in a while.

--I found them for $14.99.

--You need to see what's real.

--The bedroom is my place.

--I'm leaning towards the Jeep over the Mercedes.

--You and I can argue about that, but they don't see it the same way.

--You've got to love my day.

--He said in the email that was the only way he would talk about it.

--I said, Yep, that's it. I'm done.

--I can't do the whole belly thing.

--I don't know, it's so confusing.

--Didn't he even do a video of his place?

--That's what I was doing. I was finishing my tea.

--Do you want the front or the back?

--I hate being scared to be around people.

--We are at 28%.

--They have a huge business in Arizona.

--I heard from my neighbor on Facebook that is one of the better places to eat.

--The only reason I came was because of my friend's mom.

--When I think about it, I should be mad at Kenny.

--He doesn't deal with basics.

--If you go in the alley, it's right there.

--I saw a girl in there with a white skirt and I was like, is this a café?

--I have never been more serious.

--I actually have a job interview tomorrow.

--I cried in the coffee shop earlier.

--At least I got severance.

--(In the door) Where can I buy a puzzle?

--He has hundreds, thousands of pieces of candy.

--Richard knew from the start.

--You are doing really well.

--She helps solve mystery cases.

--I'll let you know when I'm on my way.

--I don't know what you're talking about. You'll have to point to it.

--You need a glass shelf.

--Okay, maybe I just missed them.

--It doesn't grind coffee.

--If you behave I have a surprise.

--That's what my school wants me to do, but that's not how I want to do it.

--That will keep you busy.

--The residents are after them and it became almost a threat.

--There is a video on You Tube about that.

--So then I had to drive home.

--It's not like you can wear your mask 24/7.

--I don't know where I'm going.

--The problem is Trader Joe's

--Does the drummer start with cymbals?

--Is that domestic, or what?

--She needed a room, so they moved in together.

--Come on. I'm not going to have you stop every ten feet.

--It's art. It's all that.

--Dude, it's not all about you.

--All these are flowers.

--We are not going in there.

--He is definitely on my mind.

--I got, like, an email about it.

--I'm only working four hours in the morning.

--My plan is just to bring it.

--Will you tell me what you would like to do?

--I'm starting to rethink this.

--I need to get something to eat.

--I don't exactly know how I feel about it.

--That story needs to be written.

--They've given me money to help get through a lot of this.

--Bookstores are places where you can pick up a book you might like.

--Get back to me by the first.

--I saw it from the train.

--He said he was the son, but it wasn't true.

--The problem is always the start.

--He repairs stuff because he breaks stuff.

--I've never been in there, but I'm glad it's here.

--Oh my God, I'm sorry.
    No, you're totally fine.

--You're all did up! You look cute.

--They did the hair and ring trick.

--No one is looking to us now for anything.

--It's that upper-echelon, bougie kind of vibe.

--There were 30 people in line before.

--It was based on something true.

--I can't believe I lost another water bottle.

--I had to get off. It was all wobbly.

--You should try it if you haven't.

--I have someone living with me.

--Holy Shit! A new Stephen King book.

--Sorry, I never know what day it is.

--I'm on medical leave from work.

--That makes me so irritated.
    Because it's fucking true!

--No, you're going to get me in trouble. Do not tell her!

--I love how this feels.

--They were big boys. They were a little scary.

--Make way. Make way.

--He's been bedridden.

--Maybe they just didn't get enough business.

--They are teeing off at 3:00.

--Overall it was good.

--I had high hopes for the situation, but it was too late.

--I miss going to the yoga studio. I miss the gym.

--I understand what you're saying, but that's a separate issue.

--Ride your bike in the street, not on the sidewalk.

--You need to check out their Instagram.

--I am going to have a designated goal.

--We have to find out where we're going.

--It takes her a little while, but she gets there.

--I have actually been grilling.

--The first year is the worst.

--I cannot see her waterskiing.

--Dad had to put his foot down somehow.

--You are not invincible and the virus is looking for someone to give it shelter.

--Just getting my steps in.

--Did I tell you my boss got fired?

--In my mind I'm like, why is this in vogue?

--There were flowers all around the border.

--She's a glutton for punishment. That's why she goes online.

--This is weird. I need to calculate again.

--I'll text when we get there.

--I miss you so much!

--They gave her a decent severance.

--She's said before she is an essential worker.

--There's always French onion soup.

--Stay safe.

--We are so spoiled by all this.

--That should be kept under the sink.

--The pack list was on the box.

--She has red red hair.

--They live three doors down.

--He's just been a weird little bitch since then.

--It was just like it was with you, only it was me.

--That's really corny.

--I haven't eaten it, so I don't know.

--The sooner that happens, the sooner I can say Fuck It.

--She acted like crap because she wasn't invited.

--I went to lunch with them after that, and it was not spectacular.

--They still appeal to me.

--It didn't work out?
  No, it didn't
  I knew it.

--I said I went to a bank a month ago.

--Dude, I am so angry.

--Even though I'm married, I'm like, what the hell, that's ridiculous.

--She had to wear the cone for a month.

--I actually prefer it when he's gone.

--The train is better.

--There's nothing to do but eat.

--She deserves them.

--That is not true at all.

--I'm doing my best with it, but I also don't want to be at risk.

--(In door) Do you have a bathroom in there?

--If they are not open minded, what's the fucking point?

--You seem taller.

--I'm sure there is a learning curve.

--Don't make decisions for Caitlyn. It's up to her to decide.

--I don't know what this is, but the original was so much better.

--Is he selling cars?

--You were so worried he wouldn't recognize you, but now you're okay.

--I am going to tile.

--You opened the door?
   I opened both doors.
   That's so wild.

--But you don't see any trees around.

--I was like, why is this even happening?

--I can't do noodles.

--And there's some skateboarder guy who goes around there kind of often.

--Christians are allowed to.

--I'm a lot better off because I have someone who thinks like me.

--If it had been once I wouldn't have minded.

--Yes Saturday, every Saturday.

--This is the way downtown.

--She's the worst, but she's still okay.

--I'm going to do a little cardio today.

--All that and I wasn't even there.

--I was trying to go.

--It's better than fucking IHOP, I swear.

--I can't watch any more.

--Her dogs are just so out of control.

--I know you guys do that because you told me.

--None of us knew what was coming.

--You didn't read my email, did you?

--It takes her longer to get here.

--I've been in the bar waiting.

--My boyfriend went to school there.

--What I can say is that we're hoping to finalize.

--They're becoming a thing.

--I mean, when you're there you're in the mountains, literally.

--They cancelled the entire season.

--She said it and I was like, how could you?

--I mean, they said it in a Zoom meeting for what that's worth.

--I saw it and I said, I want that.

--I think I would be a little less unhappy in California.

--So literally I had to tell him what to say.

--Every single one of them does that.

--If I play real hard, I'm happy.

--I came back and she was still asleep.

--It's always some kind of bullshit.

--If I sound like I'm walking fast, it's because I am.

--We used to spin there.

--Don't lose that. I love that.

--She got a deal because that's what she does.

--I think the employees are decreased.

--Do you want to go in?
   Do you?
   I don't know
   Okay.

--A friend of mine loved it.

--My wrist really hurt last night.

--That cost me $20,000

--Overall it's just misinformation.

--I can't do anything.

--I told them to stop. They wouldn't stop.

--People work their whole lives for that.

--Am I too old?

--I'm never anywhere.

--She's not a fan of the quarantine.

--It must only be on Saturdays.

--That is exactly what I want to do.

--That place was tacky as hell.

--Unless I love a book, I am going to get rid of it.

--Oh my god, that would be amazing.

--I've had this for 20 years, or at least 10.

--We make it 5 feet and there's another dog.

--He is never going to get over that, ever.

--Apparently you can get free Orange Theory stuff if you do it.

--Oh my God. Let's buy this!

--They said my situation was very unique.

--You could tell he wasn't smiling.

--Where is the nearest bathroom?

--It's really factual.

--I need the charger.

--Stop getting on me because I'm annoying.

--They connected me with Ashley from account services.

--I'm more intuitive.

--She saw it as sudden, but I was expecting it.

--Oh my God, that's my nightmare.

--If she had called I would have had one.

--That would be hard over time.

--(In door.) Glad to see you're still open.

--I like books, but I don't necessarily like to read them.

--I'm using the blue one because the other one broke.

--The whole town just stopped.

--He's never free in the evenings.

--They've been together for 11 years.

--That's a great mask.

--We don't have to talk too much, but I'm calling about Mom's birthday.

--He's a lot.

--I feel like I'm somewhere near DePaul.

--It was just Friday. It's not like it was anything major.

--I've been using the bark collar. Am I not supposed to use that?

--If I go to the beach, is it worth it?

--I enjoy being supportive.

--Just take the dog on a walk.

--Are you crazy? We just went to the gym.

--My ass is rusty.

--Whenever he needs to come, he'll come.

--The reality is, we provide the service.

--Would you walk at my pace?

--All this school business is nonsense.

--That's okay, as long as you don't have COVID.

--Should we see what's here?

--Enough! I'm tired of this.

--Yes, I see you right now. Straight ahead.

--You're walking weird.
   Something bit me.

--That mattered to them?
   Yeah

--First of all, that girl didn't do shit.

--It wouldn't be the first time she lied about something like that.

--You have to break me.

--I haven't been a regular smoker since Grace.

--I just don't like this whole 'tech thing' they've got going.

--I heard this super interesting podcast.

--Just go put it down.

--His place is like a dorm room.

--I can give that an hour today.

--I'm ready to go back and hibernate.

--They use a big Q-Tip.

--You're good, keep going.

--I'm sure we can fit a lot more on the roof.

--(In door) Do you buy books?

--They told me what I had to be.

--What do they call it when they get rid of hair?

--Something is always the best thing on TV.

--Don't tell anyone we spoke.

--I made chicken and asparagus.

--It's a total coming of age thing.

--I am leaning more towards a trailer.

--It was at this place, I don't even remember what it was called.

--They always talk about their boat.

--They're the worst.

--He would never do that.

--It says here this is not a life saving device.

--How many hours am I allowed to park here?

--That is the hottest thing right now.

--They can do it, but at a higher rate.

--If you are in it to feel better, it's great.

--I am so sick of this.

--(In door) Do you have used books?

--Literally every plan I have had in life has fallen through.

--She was pushing the stroller with her feet.

--Just egg whites.

--That is their problem.

--I don't understand why you wouldn't have just waited for me.

--He sees me and he runs halfway down the hallway.

--We all have a different password.

--That is a business matter.

--Oh my God! Did you see that poop?

--At the end of the day they are usually trying to get rid of their shit.

--I could read the highlighted area either way.

--I don't care about the car behind me.

--Can you talk or are you busy?

--The woman yelling was the one out of line.

--This rain is going to get us wet.

--They are complete strangers.
    Not anymore apparently.

--It was not a great encounter.

--They don't even know me, but that's okay.

--Maybe you will and maybe you won't. Either way it's up to you.

--You had a blueberry crumble for breakfast.

--I haven't been down here in so long.

--Almond milk is so watery.

--I made him try it, but I said you can spit it out if you want.

--Fuck it. No worries.

--You were very good, all things considered.

--It's about educational resources for women.

--I'm like, who cares about all that?

--There is always something there.

--You've got to make some allowances.

--You are all very far away from me right now.

--If we have all the stuff we can do it on Sunday.

--I'm open like that.

--I'm going to hop in the car, okay?

--It's unbelievable.

--I prefer spending my time on things that are a bit more productive.

--Instead of complaining, she needs to do something.

--Hotter is good.

--Go around on the right. Go around on the right.

--Is it on Netflix?

--I did not want any of this to happen.

--That's like something I would say.

--I've heard that story.

--The only reason that might be true is because he's friends with both Henry and Brandon.

--All of a sudden shit got real.

--Maybe I'll make that my next book club book.

--It's only going to get worse.

--I sympathize; I'm terrible at parallel parking.

--It's a replica.

--I don't think they are going to reopen.

--I can't see you. I can't see you.

--Three days of food. Three days of everything.

--There's a reason it is the way it is.

--I would be cautious
   You would?
   Yes.

--Brian cannot come until they clear the alley.

--I can never sit in my office all day. I have to go downstairs or take a walk.

--Am I half bad or half mad?

--I only have it on me for 15 minutes, max.

--People are going there, and they shouldn't.

--I don't want to argue about this, but I will if we talk about it.

--The bread was stale.

--Oh hell no girl.

--You have got to watch it. It's completely you.

--I had no idea she was getting engaged.

--Her glasses broke? She should definitely tell someone.

--One night you should come over for pizza and a drink.

--How bad can it be?

--Not that I need more clutter right now.

--I don't want to think about that.
   Then you shouldn't.

-- I know. It's like everything happened.

--This is the worst.

--I have not seen him in ages.

--She needs to drop that.

--Next time they need me, we'll see.

--I'm sure they have that here.

--Everyone is in a similar boat.

--I have three bathing suits. How many do you have?

--Stop your crying. Bye.

--Is it okay to park here?

--It was so cute that I bought one too.

--I've seen it at least five times.

--His whole family is stupid.

--I'm not going to kneel down and smell it.

--Going to the airport and there were all these people getting off the planes without masks and not making a big deal out of it. I'm stressed.

--I can't even listen to it.

--It's bad that it's not over.

--There was a panel on it.

--Once I get everything together, that will be all I'll need.

--People are feeling it.

--If you're going to wear spandex at least wear a different style.

--His whole life was his job.

--He's moving?

--Have you done your workout?

--It wasn't as good as the original.

--By the time I got home, I forgot.

--No, I do absolutely nothing.

--Either she comes with me or I move out on my own.

--You are screaming at me.

--I'm glad I ran into you. Thanks for texting.

--Instead of this he said he would do, you know, whatever.

--I'd like to receive workout yoga pants.

--Excuse me. I was warning you not to get out of line.

--All right, talk to you later, man.

--There is so much to read.

--Why would they not work with you?

--He's the only one I block.

--I need to rethink so many things.

--Some of it I can't get on board with.

--They literally drove it from the factory to where I was living.

--He said don't snore too loud, and I said, okay.

--I know and I treat him amazingly.

--What's your name? I always see you.

--He sees fault in him, so I don't know.

--Gardening is never like it is in the ads.

--You hurt my feelings.
   Really?
   Yes.
   Aww.

--Oh my God! People actually do that?

--I need to read more.

--(Shouting in door) So, what's the protocol?

--I like her, but I don't trust her.

--Why don't you give me your number?

--(In door) Do you sell masks here?

--Just leave it outside.

--I feel like it's tonight.

--(In door) Do you sell globes? Do you know where I can get a nice globe?

--It didn't have to happen.

--(In door) Do they ticket along here?

--Your vision is so blurry that you can't do something like that without it being weird.

--It's a little like pepper, but not quite.

--If he would go they would tell him the same thing.

--How hard would it be to write a book?

--We would date if we could.

--His blood pressure is high.

--That meat was expensive!

--I'm not going to do that. This is not over.

--You actually drank it all?

--I got tested last Wednesday.

--I don't know what I'm doing.

--I'm busy just not exposing myself to people.

--He's like, I'm all about art.

--That's not something you just say.

--I know that she found out something.

--Ally will have her key. She always does.

--He's fine. He's still taking care of it. He's still psychotic.

--I can't with them anymore.

--As long as you're past the curve, you're pretty good.

--For mental health, yes.

--I felt like I was going to throw up this morning.

--You need to catch up with me and be right here.

--It was supposed to be tourist stuff with museums.

--I need to find out the schedule of that place.

--Does anybody else want a drink?

--We've been talking for over a week and we face-timed for 3 hours.

--It's big, but I can do more with it.

--No, it's like some insane Chinese/Greek fashion thing.

--You're at home, of course you're going to think about it more.

--This is perfect. This is a great morning.

--One of them just opened in Cincinnati.

--It's a block down and then a block back up.

--Are you going separately? I just want there to be enough room in the car.

--I will wait in the background to see what else is out there.

--You have to keep growing it out.

--And that's when you find your husband?

--Did you tell her where you live?

--I want some clever line about it.

--I wasn't really listening; he was just like, in the background.

--I'm 15 minutes away.

--I can't believe it was one inch too long.

--They shut it all down.

--Since the quarantine started I've been asking myself the same question.

--I'll bring a book to the park. We can grill.

--(In door) Do you sell fancy pens?

--I made a note on the plane yesterday of things I don't want to forget.

--Why are there are chicken bones everywhere?

--You need to stay away. Six feet!

--You don't say that at breakfast.

--We need to talk about it.

--It's not sanitary. No one takes care of it.

--Probably not the best timing, but amazing.

--I never said that. I never said anything like that.

--That was how I felt this week and I was like, I can't feel like this.

--I know they have that in Arizona.

--(In door) Do you sell newspapers?

--He's fine. He's dating.

--Who is going to hear us?

--She was at my place and used my bathroom.

--If this was the walk I'd be okay with it.

--They'll be travelling and eating and gassing and whatever.

--I have no problem with calling it Boystown, but I have no problem calling it something else either.

--He won't call; it's been months.

--I have the feeling that it's mostly been like, whatever.

--I bought a Frisbee, but he never plays with it.

--I've got kids, so I'm not one to judge.

--We need to get into the fucking shade.

--No one knows what she is.

--I watched the other one, not that one.

--I was nervous around her.

--So I need to do something with the other foot to make it level.

--If I was like that I would not try it.

--This used to be something else.

--Oh my God, get the fuck out of here.

--I'm bored, okay?

--But it was also like, important to me.

--We need to come back here.

--I never go this far down Broadway.

--So now we have five free ones.

--I don't even look at the women walking by anymore. It's depressing.

--How do you feel good about this?

--I think it makes sense to do what I said.

--He'll say what he needs to say.

--Was it here?
   No, it was there.

--I like their regular ice cream better.

--You're not listening; I think you're underselling yourself.

--What do we have, another mile?

--Whatever you need, get it.

--She would not be in the picture that much if we didn't live in Chicago.

--I do think like that, and then I'm like, sad.

--That wasn't how it was when he was there.

--Why are you walking away from me?

--I'm going to make my cake.

--No one can know about this.

--I'll have to run it by Eric.

--Did you go to the wedding?

--He is very famous.

--(In door) So you require masks?

--I feel like legally you should get it.

--Three hours is easy. We hang out. We have lunch. It's not a big deal.

--Oh my God, it's her — it's Martha!

--You need to watch it.

--That's fucking nothing, dude.

--This is the reason I didn't want to come.

--They are more like; we gave you everything you need to be successful, now it's up to you.

--That's not normal.

--When you start out, that's the thing.

--He's the one with the hot wife.

--Everyone have a safe trip back.

--There were three of us and I was like, Holy shit.

--That barbecue was inspired.

--He took the city ordinance or whatever and put it on the wall while we were eating the pizza.

--It's bath products, you know? Bath products.

--I plan on going regardless.

--Blah blah blah and then she just did it.

--She worried, but what's the point of that?

--I've watched everything.

--A lot happens all day.

--They come because they want the swag.

--Now it's closed, but there is talk.

--He doesn't know that I know that he's been seeing a therapist.

--In the hallway?
    Yes, in the hallway.

--I want to get there the cheapest way.

--They will judge you. They're prudish.

--I need to be around people.

--Meeting with real people is work.

--Were you across from the barn?

--Very little is there for non-members.

--We have to order a rug.

--It's like, what are you doing? That's what I'm talking about.

--We are definitely moving out.

--She gave me the recipe.

--Because, you know, everyone had a partner but me.

--I knew it would be something like that.

--You don't know the people around you, and it's closer than 6 feet.

--He's very happy working from home.

--She was two, maybe three, steps away.

--Stir crazy was last month.

--None of this has been what I expected.

--To get a book you really have to want to get a book.

--She just follows Jack around.

--You tell me when you're done with that and then we'll do something.

--He passed all of his markers so he's home.

--You did not let me finish the sentence coming out of my mouth.

--I'm not optimistic about things.

--People are like that.

--(In door) Do you sell masks in here?

--He did a great job in the back.

--What's your gut feeling?

--The rural counties are further south.

--I'm going to air hug you.

--They were talking about doing it, but you know what, that's their decision.

--Am I legal here?

--This is the bike I fell on.

--Absolutely. She's going to be brilliant at it too.

--I'll watch you play your video games, but that's it.

--I cannot believe how curly your hair is.

--It's like, an all day bar.

--Everything there will be perfectly safe.

--I didn't really try, but it was only $2.

--Not a date really, but it could be.

--I've had to hide from the camera, even going to a friend's house.

--I shouldn't care about anything at this point.

--She said I'm the director and I said, the heck with it.

--Remember the article that David sent around?

--How are you supposed to get the chain off?

--All I had was a bagel.

--My mom practically threatened her.

--I wasn't complaining, I just thought you should know.

--I can't decide
   Then you shouldn't.

--It's about being a sponsor and not just being a friend.

--Do I pay for unlimited monthly, yes!

--I'm in front of the bookstore.

--If I've got it, you've got it. If you've got it, Eddie's got it and then everybody at the boat party has got it.

--I can't believe we did this.
   I know.

--She said she was going to the beach.

--We both know someone like that.
   The same someone.

--So theoretically, they did do it.

--Then she said, "You're lying to me. Why are you lying to me?"

--(In door) Glad to see you're still around.

--This is as fat as I've ever been.

--I just need things to be normal again.
   Me too.

--She's like a goat.

--I just don't like to work out.

--I do 26 hours a week, but I need to do more.

--Well, that's what society is all about, you know?

--We are heading home. We are heading home now.

--That's not what I said.

--I wouldn't mind it being darker.

--I already own it.

--He's always early.
   And he knows better.
   Does he?

--They are at a very good college.

--Do you want to go in there?
   Why?

--It's not something you notice right away.

--Things are better, we're texting.

--That's the funniest thing I've ever seen.

--I won't find out if it is on or off until the morning I leave.

--On both legs. Gross.

--It's so boring. It's like it never ends.
   And none of it makes any sense.

About Owen Keehnen

Queer author, activist, and grassroots historian Owen Keehnen has written several fiction and nonfiction books. He is a cofounder of the LGBTQ history, arts, education organization, the Legacy Project and current serves on the board of the group. He was inducted into the Chicago LGBT Hall of Fame in 2011 and is part of the founding group dedicated to making AIDS Garden Chicago a reality. He lives in Rogers Park with his husband Carl and their dogs.

www.ingramcontent.com/pod-product-compliance
Lightning Source LLC
Chambersburg PA
CBHW070551010526
44118CB00012B/1287